YOSEMITE UNCOVERED

A KIDS GUIDE TO DISCOVERING THE WONDERS OF YOSEMITE

BRIAN THOMAS

Copyright © 2024 by Brian Thomas

All rights reserved.

No part of this book may be reproduced in any form or by any electronic or mechanical means, including information storage and retrieval systems, without written permission from the author, except for the use of brief quotations in a book review.

CONTENTS

1. WELCOME TO YOSEMITE! ... 5
   Why Yosemite is special ... 8
   Fun facts about Yosemite ... 11
   The park's name and its meaning ... 15
   First impressions for visitors ... 18

2. A JOURNEY THROUGH TIME ... 23
   How Yosemite became a national park ... 26
   Famous people who helped protect Yosemite ... 30
   Key milestones in Yosemite's story ... 33

3. THE GIANT SEQUOIAS ... 39
   Famous trees in Yosemite ... 42
   The role of the Mariposa Grove in Yosemite's ecosystem ... 45

4. YOSEMITE'S BREATHTAKING LANDMARKS ... 49
   Yosemite Falls ... 52
   Glacier Point ... 55
   How these landmarks were formed by nature ... 58

5. ANIMALS OF YOSEMITE ... 63
   Birds ... 66
   Tips for safely observing wildlife ... 69
   Fun animal facts ... 73

6. PLANTS AND HABITATS	77
Meadows: Nature's Flower Gardens	
Wildflowers to look for	81
How plants support the park's animals	84
7. ADVENTURES IN THE PARK	89
Camping in the wilderness	93
Exploring rivers and waterfalls	97
Staying safe while adventuring	100
8. PROTECTING YOSEMITE	107
Guardians of Nature	
How Your Can Help	110
Stories of successful conservation efforts	115
9. YOSEMITE FUN FACTS AND TRIVIA	121
Yosemite Falls: A Towering Wonder	
Strange natural occurrences	125
Quiz	129
10. PLANNING YOUR VISIT	135
Spring: The Season of Waterfalls	
What to bring and how to prepare	138
A checklist of must-see places and must-do activities	142
11. YOSEMITE IN YOUR IMAGINATION	147
Painting Yosemite: The Canvas of Nature	
Conclusion: Your Yosemite Adventure Awaits!	151

1
WELCOME TO YOSEMITE!

Yosemite sits in the heart of California, nestled in a region called the Sierra Nevada. The name "Yosemite" might sound unique, and that's because it comes from the Native American Miwok people who lived here long before it became a famous destination. They called this area their home, a place of deep respect and natural beauty. For them, Yosemite wasn't just a pretty place; it was sacred. Every rock, tree, and stream held a story.

But let's rewind to how Yosemite became what we know today. Over millions of years, glaciers—giant sheets of ice—slowly carved out the valleys and sculpted the cliffs. Imagine an icy bulldozer moving across the land, shaping everything in its path. Those glaciers left behind some of the most famous landmarks in Yosemite, like Half Dome and El Capitan.

Even though the glaciers have long since melted, their fingerprints are all over the park.

Fast forward a few thousand years, and humans started noticing just how special this place was. Yosemite's story took a big turn in the mid-1800s. This was a time when the gold rush was bringing lots of people to California. Among all the chaos of people searching for gold, some stumbled upon Yosemite's magical landscapes. Word spread quickly—this wasn't just another patch of wilderness; it was breathtaking.

But here's the twist: people weren't always good to Yosemite. Settlers and miners came through, and some didn't treat the land with the care it deserved. Forests were cut down, wildlife was disturbed, and sacred Native American lands were disrespected. It seemed like Yosemite's beauty might be lost forever.

Then came a man named John Muir. If Yosemite had a superhero, he'd be it. John wasn't a park ranger or a scientist; he was someone who simply loved nature. He hiked through Yosemite, camped under its starry skies, and climbed its rocky cliffs. But he didn't just enjoy the park—he fought to protect it. He wrote about Yosemite's wonders, describing them so beautifully that people around the world began to care. His words were like magic; they convinced leaders to take action.

Thanks to John Muir and others like him, Yosemite became one of the first pieces of land in the United States to be protected for everyone to enjoy. In 1864,

President Abraham Lincoln signed a law protecting Yosemite Valley and the Mariposa Grove of giant sequoias. That was just the beginning. In 1890, Yosemite officially became a national park, part of a brand-new idea to save places of incredible beauty and history.

Today, Yosemite stretches across over 1,100 square miles. That's bigger than the entire state of Rhode Island! But it's not just big—it's packed with jaw-dropping sights. Waterfalls tumble from towering cliffs, granite mountains reach into the clouds, and meadows burst with wildflowers. It's a place that makes you feel tiny but in the best way possible, like you're part of something much bigger.

But Yosemite isn't just about what you see—it's about what you feel. Imagine standing in a meadow with the scent of pine trees all around you, hearing nothing but the sound of wind in the trees and a river rushing nearby. Imagine looking up at a night sky so dark you can see millions of stars, more than you ever thought possible. That's what makes Yosemite special. It's not just a place to visit; it's a place that stays with you.

Even if you've never been to Yosemite, you might recognize some of its most famous spots. El Capitan is a giant granite wall that looks impossible to climb—but people do! Then there's Half Dome, a mountain with a shape so unique it looks like someone took a bite out of it. Yosemite Falls, one of the tallest waterfalls in North America, roars to life in the spring as snow melts from the mountains. These landmarks are like characters in Yosemite's story, each with its own personality and history.

But there's more to Yosemite than just its big-name attractions. It's home to all kinds of plants and animals, many of which you won't find anywhere else. Giant sequoia trees, some over 2,000 years old, tower above the forest like ancient guardians. Black bears roam the woods, curious but cautious. And if you're lucky, you might spot a peregrine falcon, the fastest bird in the world, zipping through the sky.

What makes Yosemite even more amazing is how it brings people together. Every year, millions of visitors from all over the world come to hike its trails, take photos of its scenery, and simply breathe in its fresh air. They come to experience what makes Yosemite unforgettable: its sense of wonder. Whether you're exploring its valleys or just sitting quietly by a stream, it's a place where you can connect with nature in a way that's hard to describe.

Why Yosemite is special

Yosemite isn't just big—it's enormous. Picture your school's playground. Now imagine that stretched out to cover mountains, valleys, rivers, and forests that go on farther than you can see. But it's not just the size that makes it special—it's what's inside that space.

Every corner of Yosemite feels like it has its own personality, its own piece of the puzzle that makes the park extraordinary.

One of Yosemite's most famous features is its granite cliffs. These cliffs aren't just big—they're colossal. El Capitan rises over 3,000 feet from the valley floor. That's like stacking ten skyscrapers on top of each other! Climbers from around the world come here to test their skills, and some even climb without ropes. It's hard to imagine, isn't it? Standing at the base of El Capitan, you might feel small, but not in a bad way. It's the kind of small that reminds you how amazing nature can be.

And then there's Half Dome. Its curved shape looks like someone took a giant ice cream scoop to the mountain. If you're brave (and very prepared), you can hike all the way to the top. But even from far away, Half Dome is a sight that stays with you. On clear days, the sunlight makes it glow like it's covered in gold. On stormy days, clouds swirl around it, making it look like a scene from a fantasy story.

Yosemite is also home to one of the tallest waterfalls in North America—Yosemite Falls. Water roars down from a height of over 2,400 feet, crashing into the rocks below. If you stand close enough, you can feel the mist on your face. It's like the waterfall is alive, roaring and thundering as if to say, "Look at me! Isn't this amazing?" In the spring, when the snow in the mountains melts, the falls are at their strongest. But even when the water slows to a trickle in late summer, Yosemite Falls is still breathtaking.

But Yosemite isn't just about towering cliffs and waterfalls—it's also about what grows there. The giant sequoias are some of the oldest and tallest trees in the world. Standing next to one feels like standing next to a piece of history. Imagine a tree that was already ancient when the pyramids were being built. That's how old some of these trees are! Walking through the Mariposa Grove of giant sequoias feels like stepping into another world. The air smells of pine, and the ground is soft with fallen needles. It's quiet, but not silent—you might hear birds chirping or the wind rustling through the leaves.

Yosemite's wildlife is another thing that makes it special. Black bears roam the forests, often searching for food but always keeping their distance from people. Deer graze in meadows, their ears flicking at every little sound. If you look up, you might see a bald eagle soaring high above or a peregrine falcon diving at incredible speeds. Yosemite is alive with creatures, big and small, all playing their part in the park's ecosystem.

The seasons in Yosemite bring their own kind of magic. In spring, the waterfalls are at their most powerful, and wildflowers blanket the meadows in colors that look like they belong in a crayon box. Summer is perfect for hiking and camping under a sky filled with stars. Fall turns the trees into a patchwork of red, orange, and yellow, and the air becomes crisp and cool. Winter covers the park in snow, turning it into a wonderland where icicles hang from cliffs and rivers freeze into glittering sculptures.

But what truly makes Yosemite special isn't just what you see—it's how it makes you feel. There's something about being in a place like this that changes you. It makes you want to stop and pay attention to the world around you. You might notice the way sunlight filters through the trees or how the rocks feel warm under your hands. You might find yourself wondering how a place like this could even exist.

Yosemite is special because it's a reminder of how incredible our planet is. It's a place where you can see what happens when nature is left to do its thing. The mountains, the rivers, the trees—they've been here long before humans, and they'll be here long after. But it's also a place that depends on people to protect it. Yosemite has been cared for by generations of people who knew how important it was to keep it wild and free.

Fun facts about Yosemite

Did you know that Yosemite has a living tree taller than the Statue of Liberty? It's true! The Grizzly Giant, one of the famous sequoias in the Mariposa Grove, stands over 200 feet tall and has been growing for around 2,000 years. If trees could talk, imagine the stories this one could tell. It's been alive through ancient civilizations, revolutions, and the founding of the United States. Its branches are so wide you could park several cars on one of them—though that's definitely not allowed!

Yosemite is also home to one of the most jaw-dropping natural phenomena on the planet: the Firefall. No, it's not actual fire. It's a trick of the light that happens every February when Horsetail Fall glows bright orange during sunset. The waterfall looks like molten lava pouring down the cliff. This happens because of the angle of the sun at that time of year. People from all over the world come to see this dazzling display, and if you ever get the chance, it's worth the wait.

Speaking of waterfalls, Yosemite Falls doesn't just look incredible—it's also a world record holder. When it's flowing at full strength, it's the tallest waterfall in North America and one of the tallest in the world, standing at 2,425 feet. That's about as tall as 50 school buses stacked on top of each other! The falls have three sections: the Upper Fall, the Middle Cascades, and the Lower Fall. Each one is stunning on its own, but together, they create a thundering masterpiece.

Yosemite's animals have their own cool facts, too. Black bears are one of the most famous residents of the park, but did you know their fur can be brown, blonde, or even cinnamon-colored? Despite their name, not all black bears are actually black! They're excellent tree climbers and often climb to find food or to get away from danger. But don't worry—they're usually more interested in berries and insects than in bothering humans.

Another fascinating creature in Yosemite is the great gray owl. It's one of the largest owls in North America and can be found in the park's meadows and forests. These owls have incredible hearing—they can hear a mouse moving under two feet of snow! Imagine being that good at listening. It's one of the reasons they're such excellent hunters.

Yosemite isn't just about the present; it has an ancient past. The granite cliffs, like El Capitan and Half Dome, are some of the oldest rocks in the world. They formed about 100 million years ago during the time of dinosaurs. But here's the twist: those cliffs weren't always exposed. They were hidden underground until millions of years of erosion revealed them. It's like nature's version of unwrapping a gift.

And then there's the name "Yosemite." It has an interesting story, too. While many people think it means "grizzly bear" in the Miwok language, it actually refers to the people who lived in the valley. The Miwok called it "Ahwahnee," which means "big mouth," describing the shape of the valley. The word Yosemite came later, and while it's not the original name, it stuck.

Even Yosemite's weather is fascinating. While summers can be warm and sunny, winters are a completely different story. Snow blankets the park, transforming it into a wonderland. Some years, enough snow piles up to create natural bridges across streams, and parts of the Merced River freeze solid enough for ice skaters. But even in winter, certain spots, like the Mist Trail, stay green and lively thanks to the flowing water that never stops.

Here's another fun fact: Yosemite is home to a very unusual natural sound. It's called a rockfall roar. Yosemite's steep cliffs sometimes release chunks of granite, sending them tumbling down the mountainside. When this happens, it creates a rumbling sound that can echo across the valley. It's not dangerous if you're far enough away, but it's definitely a reminder of the park's powerful geology.

Stars over Yosemite are also something special. On a clear night, you can see the Milky Way stretching across the sky, along with shooting stars and planets. There's almost no light pollution in the park, which means the stars shine brighter than most people have ever seen. If you ever get to visit, lying on your back in a meadow and staring up at the sky is an experience you won't forget.

For those who love climbing, Yosemite is a paradise. El Capitan is one of the most challenging climbs in the world, but did you know someone climbed it in less than four hours without any ropes? His name is Alex Honnold, and his climb in 2017 was so daring it became the subject of an award-winning movie. Climbers from around the world come to Yosemite to test their skills on its famous cliffs, making it a hub for adventure and bravery.

Even the rivers in Yosemite have their own stories. The Merced River, which winds through the valley, is not just a pretty sight—it's essential to the ecosystem. It provides water for plants and animals and creates sandy beaches perfect for picnics and relaxing. During spring, when the snow melts, the river swells and becomes a rushing force of nature, perfect for rafting.

If you think Yosemite is only about natural beauty, think again. It has inspired artists, writers, and photographers for over a century. Ansel Adams, one of the most famous photographers in the world, took some of his most iconic pictures in Yosemite. His black-and-white photos of Half Dome and Bridalveil Fall are legendary, capturing the park's grandeur in a way words sometimes can't.

The park's name and its meaning

What's in a name? When it comes to Yosemite, a name holds a story, a history, and even a little bit of mystery. Saying "Yosemite" feels like stepping into an adventure. But have you ever stopped to wonder what it means or where it came from? The name wasn't just plucked out of thin air—it's tied to the land, the people who lived here, and even a few bears.

Long before the name "Yosemite" appeared on

maps, this land was home to Native American tribes, including the Miwok people. To them, it wasn't called Yosemite. It was known as "Ahwahnee," which means "big mouth." Now, this might sound strange at first, but if you imagine standing in Yosemite Valley, surrounded by towering granite cliffs, it starts to make sense. The valley's wide, open shape resembles a giant mouth. For the Miwok people, this name described not only the land but also its importance as a place to live, hunt, and tell stories.

But how did "Ahwahnee" become "Yosemite"? That's where things get a little more complicated—and interesting. During the 1800s, when European-American settlers began exploring and claiming lands in California, they encountered the Native Americans living in the valley. Unfortunately, this wasn't a peaceful meeting. Conflicts broke out, and the settlers began using the name "Yosemite" to refer to the people they encountered. They believed "Yosemite" meant "grizzly bear," referring to the Miwok tribe's skill as hunters and their connection to the animals of the land.

But here's the twist: the Miwok didn't call themselves Yosemite. In fact, the name likely came from a misunderstanding. It seems the word "Yosemite" was the settlers' version of a Miwok word that meant "those who kill." It wasn't meant to be a compliment. It was a term used by neighboring tribes to describe the people who lived in the valley—possibly as a warning about their strength and fierceness in protecting their home. Over time, the name "Yosemite" stuck, not for the people but for the land itself.

Even though the name's origins are tied to conflict, it's also a reminder of how powerful and enduring the connection to this land is. The Miwok people saw Yosemite as more than just a home. It was a place of deep spiritual significance. They believed the towering cliffs and flowing rivers were created by powerful forces and that every part of the land had a purpose and a story. For them, nature wasn't separate from life —it was life.

One of the most fascinating legends from the Miwok people involves the creation of Yosemite's cliffs. According to their stories, long ago, two mischievous bear cubs climbed up a steep rock face and got stuck at the top. Their mother, desperate to rescue them, called on the animal spirits for help. The spirits stretched the rock higher and higher, creating the giant cliffs of El Capitan. The cubs were saved, and the cliffs remained as a reminder of the event.

The story of Yosemite's name is also a story about how language and culture shape the way we see the world. To the Miwok people, the valley was Ahwahnee, a place filled with meaning and life. To the settlers, it became Yosemite, a name that eventually came to represent one of the most beautiful places in the world. Even though the name has changed, the land itself remains as extraordinary as ever.

But what about the bears? If the name "Yosemite" is connected to the idea of grizzly bears, does that mean there are grizzlies in the park today? The answer is no—at least not anymore. Grizzly bears once roamed Yosemite, but they disappeared from the region in the early 1900s due to hunting and habitat loss. Today, the bears you'll find in Yosemite are black bears. Despite their name, black bears come in a variety of colors, including brown and cinnamon. They're smaller and less aggressive than grizzlies, but they're still a big part of Yosemite's story.

The meaning of Yosemite has grown over time. It's no longer just a name tied to its early history—it's become a symbol of natural beauty and the importance of protecting wild places. For millions of people who visit every year, "Yosemite" means adventure, discovery, and awe. It's a place where you can walk among ancient trees, stand at the base of thunderous waterfalls, and feel connected to something bigger than yourself.

First impressions for visitors

One of the first things people notice is how big everything feels. The granite cliffs tower over you, so massive it's hard to believe they're real. There's El Capitan, rising straight up from the valley floor like a stone skyscraper, and then there's Half Dome, its rounded top almost glowing in the sunlight. These formations aren't just landmarks; they're like characters in Yosemite's story, standing silently but speaking volumes about the power of nature.

For many visitors, the journey begins at a spot called Tunnel View. It's a famous overlook, and for good reason. When you step out of your car or take a few steps down the path, it hits you: the view stretches out like a postcard brought to life. You can see Bridalveil Fall spilling down one side, El Capitan on the other, and in the distance, the rounded peak of Half Dome. It's the kind of sight that makes people gasp, and it's a moment you never forget.

There's a reason why people often call Yosemite "awe-inspiring." It's because awe is exactly what you feel. It's not just about seeing something beautiful—it's about feeling something. Your heart might beat a little faster, or you might stand there quietly, taking it all in. For some, it's the way the sunlight dances on the rocks. For others, it's the sheer scale of the cliffs, so big they make you feel small in the best way. It's not just scenery; it's an experience.

As you get closer to the valley floor, new details start to come into focus. The Merced River winds its way through the meadows, reflecting the cliffs and trees like a mirror. Deer graze nearby, their ears twitching as they listen for sounds you can't even hear. Birds dart between the trees, their calls echoing in the cool morning air. Everything feels alive, and you can't help but feel alive, too.

For many visitors, the waterfalls are a highlight of their first visit. In the spring, when the snow melts, the waterfalls roar with so much power you can hear them before you see them. Yosemite Falls, one of the tallest waterfalls in North America, tumbles down the cliffs in three stages, and the sound is like thunder. If you get close enough, the mist from the falls might hit your face, a cool and refreshing reminder of nature's strength. It's not just something you see—it's something you feel.

One of the surprising things about Yosemite is how quiet it can be. Even with other visitors around, there are moments when all you hear is the rustle of leaves or the distant sound of water. It's the kind of quiet that makes you notice things you might otherwise miss, like the way the light changes as clouds move across the sky or the tiny details of a wildflower blooming by the trail.

Another first impression many people have is just how much there is to explore. It's not just the big landmarks like El Capitan or Yosemite Falls—though those are unforgettable—it's also the smaller, hidden places. Maybe it's a shaded grove of trees where sunlight filters through the branches, or a rocky stream where the water is so clear you can see the pebbles at the bottom. Every turn feels like it could lead to something new, and that sense of discovery is part of what makes Yosemite so special.

Even the air feels different in Yosemite. It's cool,

crisp, and carries the scent of pine, wildflowers, and sometimes even the faint smell of wood smoke from a distant campfire. Taking a deep breath here feels different, like you're breathing in the wildness of the park itself. It's a small thing, but it's something visitors often remember long after they've left.

And then there's the light. Morning light spills into the valley, turning the cliffs gold and the meadows green. As the sun rises higher, the light shifts, making the granite shimmer or casting long, dramatic shadows. Sunset is its own kind of magic, painting the sky with shades of pink, orange, and purple while the cliffs seem to glow from within. Even after the sun sets, the show isn't over. On clear nights, the stars come out in full force, blanketing the sky in a way that city-dwellers might find hard to believe. It's like the park has its own natural spotlight, highlighting its beauty at every hour.

2

A JOURNEY THROUGH TIME

Before Yosemite became a national park or even had a name like Yosemite, it was already a home. Long before roads, campgrounds, or tourists, the valley and its surrounding lands belonged to Native American tribes. For them, this place wasn't just a beautiful landscape—it was life itself. Every tree, river, and mountain held meaning. This connection shaped how they lived, worked, and understood the world.

The first people to call Yosemite home were the Ahwahneechee, a group descended from the larger Miwok tribe. They named the valley "Ahwahnee," which means "big mouth." Standing in the middle of the valley, surrounded by cliffs like El Capitan and Half Dome, you can imagine why. The shape of the land felt like a protective enclosure—a big mouth holding everything precious inside. For the Ahwahneechee, the valley wasn't just a place to live; it was a sacred space.

Life here revolved around nature. The Ahwahneechee didn't build large cities or clear the land for farming the way some other tribes did. Instead, they lived in harmony with the land, taking only what they needed. They built their homes, called umachas, using cedar bark and other natural materials. These small, dome-shaped structures blended into the landscape, leaving little trace on the environment.

One of their main sources of food was acorns, which came from the black oak trees that still grow in Yosemite today. Gathering acorns wasn't as simple as just picking them up and eating them. The process took skill and patience. The Ahwahneechee would collect acorns in the fall, dry them out, and then grind them into a fine powder using stone tools. The powder was leached with water to remove the bitterness, turning it into a nutritious meal. This acorn flour was a staple in their diet and could be stored for months, helping them survive through the winter.

But food wasn't just about survival—it was also about community. The Ahwahneechee would often gather together for meals, storytelling, and ceremonies. These gatherings were an important way to pass down knowledge from one generation to the next. Elders would tell stories about the land, the animals, and the spirits that watched over them. These stories weren't just entertainment—they were lessons. They taught younger members of the tribe how to respect the land and live in balance with it.

One of the most well-known stories from the Ahwahneechee involves the creation of Half Dome. According to legend, it was once a giant rock spirit that lived peacefully in the valley. One day, it got into a terrible fight with another spirit, causing a piece of it to be broken off. The jagged edge you see today is a reminder of that battle. For the Ahwahneechee, this wasn't just a tale—it was a way of explaining the world around them and understanding their place in it.

The animals of Yosemite were also deeply respected. The Ahwahneechee believed that every creature had a spirit and a purpose. Bears, for example, were seen as powerful and wise. They inspired both fear and admiration. If an Ahwahneechee hunter encountered a bear, it wasn't just a random meeting—it was a significant moment. The hunter would perform a ritual to honor the bear's spirit, whether or not it was hunted for food. This respect for animals ensured that the Ahwahneechee never took more than they needed and always gave thanks for what the land provided.

While the Ahwahneechee were the main inhabitants of Yosemite Valley, other Native American tribes also visited the area. The Mono Lake Paiute people, who lived to the east, would trade with the Ahwahneechee, bringing goods like obsidian for making tools. These exchanges weren't just about trading items—they were also a way of sharing knowledge and forming alliances. Together, the tribes created a network of connections that stretched far beyond the valley.

But life in Yosemite wasn't always peaceful. The Ahwahneechee had to defend their home from rival tribes and, later, from settlers who arrived in the mid-1800s during the California Gold Rush. These settlers brought disease, disrupted hunting grounds, and claimed land that had been sacred for generations. The Ahwahneechee fought to protect their home, but the arrival of the settlers changed their way of life forever.

By the late 1800s, many Ahwahneechee people were forced to leave Yosemite. Some were relocated to reservations, while others tried to adapt to the new world brought by settlers. Despite these challenges, the Ahwahneechee and other Native American tribes didn't disappear. Their descendants continue to honor their connection to Yosemite today, sharing their traditions, stories, and knowledge with those who visit the park.

How Yosemite became a national park

In the mid-1800s, big changes were happening in California. The Gold Rush had brought thousands of people westward, all hoping to strike it rich. Among the hustle and chaos, Yosemite remained a quiet, untouched valley. Then, in 1851, a group called the Mariposa Battalion arrived in Yosemite Valley during a campaign against the Native American tribes in the region. When these settlers saw the towering cliffs and waterfalls for the first time, they were stunned. They had never seen anything like it. It wasn't gold they had found, but something far more valuable—though it would take years for most people to realize it.

One of the first people to truly appreciate Yosemite's beauty was a man named James Mason Hutchings. He wasn't a scientist or a politician—he was a publisher. Hutchings visited Yosemite in 1855 and was so amazed that he decided to tell the world about it. He wrote articles and published some of the earliest illustrations of Yosemite, showing its cliffs, waterfalls, and giant sequoia trees. For many people living far away, Hutchings' work was their first glimpse of Yosemite. His writings and drawings sparked curiosity, making people wonder what it would be like to stand in the shadow of El Capitan or hear the roar of Yosemite Falls.

But Hutchings wasn't just interested in showing off Yosemite. He wanted to profit from it, too. He began leading tours into the valley, building lodges for visitors, and even claiming land in Yosemite for himself. Back then, there were no laws protecting the land, so settlers like Hutchings felt free to take what they wanted. While he helped spread the word about Yosemite's beauty, his actions also raised an important question: Should a place like Yosemite belong to private individuals, or should it be protected for everyone?

Around the same time, another man was falling in love with Yosemite in a completely different way. His name was Galen Clark. Clark wasn't interested in making money from Yosemite; he was more interested in saving it. After moving to the area for health reasons, he became fascinated by the giant sequoias in the Mariposa Grove. He spent hours exploring the forest, marveling at the size and age of the trees. Clark believed these trees were more than just impressive—they were treasures that needed to be preserved.

Clark wasn't alone in thinking this way. As more settlers arrived and the impact of tourism grew, people began to worry that Yosemite's natural beauty might be destroyed. Trees were being cut down, wildlife was being hunted, and the land was being altered to make room for buildings and roads. Something had to be done to protect Yosemite before it was too late.

That's where Abraham Lincoln comes into the story. In 1864, during the middle of the Civil War, President Lincoln signed a bill called the Yosemite Grant. This was a groundbreaking moment—it was the first time in American history that land was set aside by the federal government to be preserved for public use. The Yosemite Grant protected Yosemite Valley and the Mariposa Grove, ensuring that they would remain untouched by private ownership or development. The land was given to the state of California, with the promise that it would be managed for the benefit of everyone.

But the Yosemite Grant didn't protect the entire area we now think of as Yosemite National Park. It was a good start, but much of the surrounding wilderness was still at risk. That's where John Muir came in. Muir was a naturalist, writer, and one of the greatest advocates for Yosemite. He first visited the valley in 1868, and it changed his life. Muir believed that nature was sacred, and he spent years exploring Yosemite, studying its ecosystems, and writing about its wonders.

Muir's writings captured the hearts of people all over the world. He described Yosemite with such passion and detail that readers felt like they were standing right there with him, looking up at Half Dome or wandering through the Mariposa Grove. But Muir didn't just want people to admire Yosemite from afar—he wanted them to understand why it needed to be protected.

One of Muir's biggest challenges was convincing the government to take action. At the time, many people believed that natural resources should be used for economic growth, not preserved for beauty. Muir argued that places like Yosemite were more valuable left untouched. He wrote articles, gave speeches, and even hosted famous guests, like President Theodore Roosevelt, who joined Muir on a camping trip in

Yosemite in 1903. During this trip, Muir showed Roosevelt the damage being done to the park and urged him to expand its protections.

Roosevelt was impressed. In 1906, he signed a law that took Yosemite Valley and the Mariposa Grove away from California and placed them under federal protection. This decision created Yosemite National Park as we know it today, ensuring that it would be preserved not just for the people of California, but for the entire nation.

Famous people who helped protect Yosemite

John Muir wasn't the first person to care about Yosemite, but he's one of the most famous. Born in Scotland in 1838, Muir grew up surrounded by the rugged beauty of his homeland. When he was 11, his family moved to the United States, and he spent much of his youth exploring the forests and fields near his new home in Wisconsin. Muir was endlessly curious about the world. He loved climbing trees, studying plants, and inventing gadgets—once, he built a clock that also worked as a machine to wake him up in the morning.

But Muir's life wasn't always about nature. For a while, he worked in factories, making machines and tools. Then, an accident nearly blinded him. As he recovered, Muir realized how much he missed the beauty of the natural world. He made a promise to himself: he would dedicate his life to exploring and protecting nature. That promise eventually brought him to Yosemite in 1868.

When Muir first arrived in Yosemite, he was overwhelmed by its beauty. He hiked through its valleys, climbed its cliffs, and spent nights sleeping under the stars. The more time he spent in Yosemite, the more he believed it was a place worth protecting. But at that time, not everyone agreed. Many people thought nature was only valuable if it could be turned into money—through mining, logging, or farming. Muir saw things differently. He believed Yosemite had value simply because it was wild and beautiful.

Muir wasn't just a hiker and a nature lover—he was also a writer. He wrote essays and books about Yosemite, describing its cliffs, trees, and waterfalls in ways that made people feel like they were right there with him. He called the sequoias "the noblest of a noble race," and described the sound of Yosemite Falls as "music that never dies." His words inspired readers to see nature not as something to be tamed, but as something to be cherished.

One of Muir's most famous essays was about the giant sequoias in the Mariposa Grove. These trees, some over 2,000 years old, were being cut down to make fences and buildings. Muir argued that these ancient giants deserved to be protected, not destroyed. His essays reached people all over the country, and they began to see Yosemite as a place worth saving.

Muir wasn't alone in his efforts. Another important figure in Yosemite's story was Galen Clark, a settler who also fell in love with the park's beauty. Clark was one of the first people to call for the protection of Yosemite Valley and the Mariposa Grove. He became the park's first "guardian," a role similar to what we'd now call a park ranger. Clark's quiet dedication inspired others, including Muir, to fight for Yosemite's preservation.

But Muir wasn't just writing essays and hiking through the wilderness. He also worked to get powerful people involved in protecting Yosemite. One of those people was President Theodore Roosevelt. Roosevelt was an outdoorsman himself, and he admired Muir's passion for nature. In 1903, Muir invited Roosevelt to camp in Yosemite. The two men spent three days exploring the park, hiking through the Mariposa Grove and sleeping under the stars near Glacier Point. During their trip, Muir explained why Yosemite needed federal protection—not just to save its cliffs and trees, but to ensure it remained wild for future generations.

That camping trip worked. Roosevelt was deeply moved by what he saw and heard. In 1906, he signed a law that placed Yosemite Valley and the Mariposa Grove under federal protection, making them part of Yosemite National Park. This was a huge victory for Muir and everyone who had worked to save the park.

But Yosemite's story didn't end there. Over the

years, other people have played important roles in protecting and managing the park. One of them was Ansel Adams, a photographer who captured Yosemite's beauty in black-and-white images that became famous around the world. Adams' photographs helped raise awareness about Yosemite's importance, inspiring even more people to care about the park.

Then there's Florence Hutchings, a young girl who lived in Yosemite during the late 1800s. Known as "Floy," she loved exploring the valley and was one of its most enthusiastic champions. Even though she wasn't famous like Muir or Adams, her love for Yosemite showed that you don't have to be a grown-up or a celebrity to make a difference. Her stories remind us that anyone can fall in love with a place like Yosemite—and that love can inspire others.

Key milestones in Yosemite's story

Let's go back to 1864. Imagine the United States during the Civil War—a time when the country was deeply divided, with battles raging and many people focused on survival. It might seem like the worst possible time to think about saving a patch of wilderness in California. But that's exactly when something extraordinary happened. President Abraham Lincoln signed the Yosemite Grant, setting aside Yosemite Valley and the Mariposa Grove of giant sequoias as protected land.

This was the first time in American history that land was preserved for public use and enjoyment. It was a revolutionary idea: the government recognizing that nature wasn't just something to be used, but something to be saved for everyone.

Even with this new protection, Yosemite wasn't entirely safe. The Yosemite Grant only covered the valley and the Mariposa Grove, leaving much of the surrounding wilderness vulnerable. That's where John Muir came in. Muir wasn't just a lover of Yosemite—he was its fiercest defender. By the late 1800s, his essays and books had convinced people that Yosemite wasn't just a beautiful place; it was a vital part of the natural world that needed protection. His efforts led to another major milestone in 1890: the creation of Yosemite National Park. This expanded the protected area to include the high country surrounding the valley, adding the breathtaking peaks, meadows, and rivers we know today.

But even with the national park designation, Yosemite's challenges weren't over. In the early 1900s, there was still a gap between the state-controlled Yosemite Valley and the federally managed national park land around it. This split caused confusion about how the park should be run and left parts of it open to exploitation. Enter President Theodore Roosevelt. After his famous camping trip with John Muir in 1903, Roosevelt was determined to unify the park under federal control. In 1906, he made it happen, transferring Yosemite Valley and the Mariposa Grove to the federal government. This brought the entire park together under one system, ensuring it could be managed and protected as a whole.

While these legal milestones were important, Yosemite's story isn't just about laws—it's also about people who fell in love with the park and worked to share its beauty with the world. One of those people was Ansel Adams, a photographer whose images of Yosemite became iconic. Starting in the 1920s, Adams used his camera to capture the park's cliffs, waterfalls, and forests in breathtaking detail. His black-and-white photographs showed Yosemite in a way that words couldn't, inspiring people who had never seen the park to care about it. Adams' work wasn't just art—it was advocacy, helping to strengthen the movement to preserve Yosemite for future generations.

Another key moment came in 1964, exactly 100 years after the Yosemite Grant. That year, the United States passed the Wilderness Act, which aimed to protect wild areas across the country. Yosemite was a big part of this effort. Large sections of the park were designated as wilderness areas, meaning they would be kept free from roads, buildings, and other developments. This helped ensure that Yosemite's most remote and untouched places would stay that way, allowing visitors to experience nature in its purest form.

But protecting Yosemite hasn't always been about

adding new laws. Sometimes, it's been about fixing mistakes from the past. In the 1990s, a major restoration project began to remove old buildings and roads from Yosemite Valley and return it to a more natural state. The goal was to make the valley look and feel more like it did before settlers arrived, giving visitors a better sense of its original beauty. This effort wasn't easy—removing structures and replanting forests took years of hard work—but it showed how much people were willing to invest in keeping Yosemite wild and free.

Not all milestones in Yosemite's story have been about preservation. Some have been about discovery. For example, in the 19th and 20th centuries, scientists began studying the park's geology, plants, and animals in greater detail. They uncovered the secrets of how Yosemite's cliffs were shaped by glaciers, how its ecosystems support a wide variety of life, and how its iconic waterfalls change with the seasons. These discoveries didn't just help scientists—they also helped visitors understand and appreciate the park in new ways.

Yosemite's milestones haven't just been about what happens inside the park. They've also influenced the world outside it. The Yosemite Grant helped inspire the creation of the national park system, an idea that has spread around the globe. Today, there are over 4,000 national parks and protected areas worldwide, all of them built on the same idea that started in

Yosemite: that some places are so special they should be preserved for everyone, forever.

Even in recent years, Yosemite continues to make history. Efforts to address climate change, manage increased tourism, and protect endangered species are shaping the park's future. Each generation faces new challenges, but the commitment to keeping Yosemite a place of beauty and wonder remains the same.

3

THE GIANT SEQUOIAS

The story of a giant sequoia starts small—really small. Picture a cone, about the size of a chicken egg. Inside that cone are dozens of tiny seeds, each no bigger than a flake of oatmeal. It's hard to believe something so small could grow into one of the largest living things on Earth, but that's exactly what happens. When the cone falls from a tree, it dries out in the sun, opening up to release its seeds. If a seed lands in just the right spot—with plenty of sunlight, water, and space—it can begin to grow into a sapling, a baby tree.

Giant sequoias are picky about where they grow. They're found only in certain parts of the world, and Yosemite is one of those special places. They need the perfect combination of a high-altitude climate, rich soil, and plenty of water. These trees are like nature's Goldilocks—they need everything to be "just right."

That's why you'll only find them in small groves, tucked into the Sierra Nevada mountains.

Once a sapling starts growing, it doesn't waste any time. During its first few years, it shoots upward, reaching for the sunlight. But what's happening below ground is just as important. A giant sequoia's roots spread out wide—sometimes stretching over 100 feet from the base of the tree. These roots anchor the tree firmly in place, helping it stand tall even during strong winds and heavy snowstorms. Unlike some other trees, giant sequoias don't have a deep taproot. Instead, their strength comes from their wide, shallow root system that works like a network to keep them steady.

As the years go by, the sequoia keeps growing. Its trunk thickens, its branches stretch out, and its bark becomes thicker and more rugged. The bark is one of the reasons giant sequoias can live so long. It's not just thick—it's also full of tannins, a chemical that makes the bark resistant to insects, diseases, and even fire. When a wildfire sweeps through the forest, the thick bark protects the tree, and the heat can actually help open the cones, releasing more seeds to start the next generation of trees.

Fire might sound like a bad thing, but for giant sequoias, it's a natural part of their life cycle. Fires clear out smaller plants and debris on the forest floor, giving sequoia seeds a better chance to take root. They also create nutrient-rich soil, which helps the saplings grow strong. It's like nature's way of hitting the reset button, ensuring the forest stays healthy and vibrant.

What's even more amazing is how long these trees can keep growing. Some giant sequoias are over 3,000 years old. Think about that for a moment. These trees were already ancient when the pyramids of Egypt were being built. They've stood through countless storms, fires, and even earthquakes. How do they do it? Part of the answer lies in their incredible ability to repair themselves. If a branch breaks or part of the trunk is damaged, the tree can heal itself, growing new wood to cover the wound. This resilience helps them survive challenges that would kill other trees.

But why are giant sequoias so tall? A lot of it has to do with their location and the conditions they grow in. High in the mountains, there's plenty of sunlight and water, which are essential for photosynthesis. Photosynthesis is how trees turn sunlight into food, and giant sequoias are especially good at it. Their massive size allows them to capture more sunlight than smaller trees, giving them an edge in the competition for resources.

Their height is also a defense mechanism. By growing taller than other trees, sequoias can reach sunlight even in crowded forests. Their towering branches also make it harder for animals to reach their cones, ensuring that only a few seeds fall to the ground to grow into new trees.

Despite their size, giant sequoias are surprisingly

light. Their wood is less dense than many other trees, which helps them grow taller without collapsing under their own weight. This combination of strength and lightness is what allows them to reach heights of over 300 feet.

Walking through a grove of giant sequoias, it's hard not to feel small—and that's part of their magic. These trees remind us of how vast and powerful nature can be. They've been standing in the same spot for thousands of years, watching the world change around them. And yet, they keep growing, reaching for the sky, year after year.

Every giant sequoia has its own story, written in its rings. If you were to cut through the trunk of a fallen tree (which is something we leave to scientists, of course), you'd see rings that tell its history. Each ring represents a year of growth, and the size of the rings can reveal what conditions were like in a particular year. A wide ring might mean there was plenty of rain, while a narrow ring could indicate a drought. These trees are living time capsules, holding the history of the forest in their trunks.

Famous trees in Yosemite

The Grizzly Giant isn't just big—it's enormous. Its trunk is over 25 feet wide. Imagine a classroom with walls as far apart as that tree's base. That's how large it is. Its tallest branch alone is thicker than most regular trees, and yet it's just one part of this ancient giant. Scientists estimate the Grizzly Giant is over 2,000 years old. It's been alive longer than the Roman Empire lasted, and it was already ancient when people started building castles in Europe.

But the Grizzly Giant isn't just impressive because of its size or age. It's also full of character. Look up, and you'll notice that its branches twist and bend in all kinds of directions. Some point straight out, like arms frozen mid-wave. Others droop under their own weight, as though the tree is tired after standing tall for so many centuries. These twists and bends tell the story of the challenges the tree has faced—storms, snow, droughts—and how it's survived them all.

The Grizzly Giant isn't alone in the Mariposa Grove. Nearby, you'll find another famous tree: the California Tunnel Tree. This tree is unique because it has a giant hole carved through its base, large enough for people to walk through. The tunnel was created in the late 1800s as a way to attract visitors to Yosemite. While cutting into a tree might not sound like the best way to honor it, the practice was common at the time. Today, the California Tunnel Tree is one of the few tunnel trees still standing, and it serves as a reminder of how people's attitudes toward nature have changed over the years.

Another iconic tree in the grove is the Faithful Couple. These are actually two sequoias whose trunks have grown so close together that they've fused at the base. It's as if they're holding onto each other for support, standing tall side by side through centuries of growth. Visitors often point out how the Faithful Couple looks like a symbol of unity and resilience, a reminder that even the mightiest trees benefit from a little companionship.

If you venture deeper into the grove, you'll come across the Fallen Monarch. Unlike the other trees, this one lies on the forest floor, its massive trunk stretched out like a natural bridge. The Fallen Monarch has been down for hundreds of years, but it hasn't decayed. That's because giant sequoias have natural chemicals in their wood that resist rot and insects. Even in death, this tree contributes to the forest, providing shelter for animals and nutrients for the soil.

The Grizzly Giant and its neighbors aren't just remarkable because of their size or shapes—they're also part of a much larger story. Each tree is a living link to the past, a witness to thousands of years of history. Think about all the things that have happened during the Grizzly Giant's lifetime. It's stood through earthquakes, fires, and countless winters. It's seen the arrival of Native American tribes, the first European settlers, and millions of visitors from around the world.

But the Grizzly Giant doesn't just sit there watching history pass by. It plays an active role in its ecosystem. Its cones, filled with tiny seeds, have helped create new generations of sequoias. Its branches provide homes for animals like squirrels and birds. Even the fallen needles around its base help enrich the soil, ensuring that the forest remains healthy and vibrant.

The role of the Mariposa Grove in Yosemite's ecosystem

Giant sequoias are massive, and their branches create a canopy that provides shade for the forest floor. This shade is like nature's air conditioning. It helps keep the ground cool, which is important for the plants and animals that live there. Smaller trees, ferns, and mosses all rely on the sequoias' shade to protect them from the harsh sun. Without the canopy, the forest floor could become too dry and hot for these plants to survive.

The sequoias also play a big role in the water cycle. Their roots, which spread out wide instead of deep, help soak up rainwater and snowmelt. This water doesn't just stay in the trees—it slowly seeps into the ground, feeding streams and rivers that flow through Yosemite. In a way, the giant sequoias act like natural water towers, collecting and distributing moisture to the forest and beyond.

Then there are the cones. Have you ever picked up a giant sequoia cone? They're surprisingly small for such a huge tree, but they're packed with seeds that have the potential to grow into towering giants themselves. The Mariposa Grove produces thousands of cones every year, each one filled with seeds that can sprout into new life. But here's the catch: those seeds need a little help to get started. This is where fire comes in.

Fire might sound like the enemy of a forest, but for the Mariposa Grove, it's a friend. When a wildfire sweeps through the grove, it clears away dead plants and creates open spaces on the forest floor. These clearings are the perfect spots for sequoia seeds to take root. The heat from the fire also helps open up the cones, releasing the seeds inside. Without fire, the sequoias would struggle to reproduce, and the grove wouldn't stay healthy.

The Mariposa Grove doesn't just help plants—it's also a home for countless animals. Birds like woodpeckers make their nests in the sequoias' thick bark, while squirrels scurry around collecting seeds and cones. Black bears often wander through the grove, searching for food or a quiet place to rest. Even the tiny insects that live in the trees play an important role, breaking down dead wood and returning nutrients to the soil.

One of the most amazing things about the Mariposa Grove is how everything is connected. The sequoias depend on the soil, water, and sunlight to grow. The animals rely on the trees for shelter and food. And the smaller plants on the forest floor benefit from the shade and nutrients provided by the sequoias. It's like a giant puzzle where every piece fits together perfectly.

But the grove's role goes beyond just helping plants and animals. It also has a huge impact on people. For thousands of years, Native American tribes have visited the Mariposa Grove, drawing inspiration and wisdom from its towering trees. They saw the grove as a sacred place, where the natural world seemed closer to the spiritual one. Today, millions of visitors come to Yosemite each year, many of them heading straight to the Mariposa Grove to stand in awe of its ancient trees.

4
YOSEMITE'S BREATHTAKING LANDMARKS

Half Dome is one of the most iconic sights in Yosemite. Its curved shape makes it look like a giant dome sliced neatly in half, as if some mythical being decided to take a bite out of the mountain. Rising over 8,800 feet above sea level, it dominates the skyline, catching the sunlight during the day and glowing softly under the moonlight. But Half Dome isn't just beautiful—it's also full of mystery. Its unique shape has led to many stories and legends about how it came to be.

According to one Native American tale, Half Dome was once a full dome, standing proudly in the valley. But one day, a powerful spirit became angry and smashed part of the dome with its hand, creating the jagged edge we see today. To the people who first lived in Yosemite, Half Dome wasn't just a rock—it was a reminder of the forces of nature and the spirits that shaped their world.

In modern times, Half Dome is famous for something else: its challenging hike. For those who are brave and prepared, the journey to the top of Half Dome is an adventure unlike any other. The trail stretches for miles, winding through forests, past waterfalls, and up steep granite slopes. The final stretch is the most intense. Hikers must climb a cable route—a pair of steel cables anchored into the rock—to reach the summit. It's not for the faint of heart, but those who make it to the top are rewarded with a breathtaking view of Yosemite Valley below. Standing on the summit, it feels like you're on top of the world.

While Half Dome's curved shape feels approachable, El Capitan is the opposite. It's a sheer vertical wall of granite, rising more than 3,000 feet above the valley floor. Its name means "The Captain" in Spanish, and it truly lives up to the title. El Capitan is massive, commanding attention from anyone who sees it. Unlike Half Dome, which seems to invite people to climb it, El Capitan dares them to try.

For years, people believed El Capitan was impossible to climb. Its smooth granite face looks like a giant wall, with no obvious handholds or paths. But in 1958, a group of climbers proved that impossible wasn't a word they believed in. Using ropes, pitons, and sheer determination, Warren Harding, Wayne Merry, and George Whitmore became the first people to scale El

Capitan's Nose route. Their climb took 47 days, spread out over a year, and it changed the world of rock climbing forever.

Today, El Capitan is considered one of the greatest climbing challenges on Earth. Climbers from all over the world come to Yosemite to test their skills on its towering walls. Some take days to ascend, sleeping in hanging tents called portaledges that dangle high above the ground. Others, like Alex Honnold, have taken a different approach. In 2017, Honnold made history by climbing El Capitan without any ropes or safety gear, a feat called free soloing. His climb took less than four hours, and it's widely regarded as one of the most daring achievements in climbing history.

But you don't have to be a climber to enjoy El Capitan. Many visitors to Yosemite simply marvel at its size and beauty from the valley floor. On sunny days, you can often spot climbers inching their way up the wall, looking like tiny ants against the massive granite surface. During the evening, El Capitan catches the light of the setting sun, turning shades of gold and pink before fading into the night.

Both Half Dome and El Capitan are made of granite, a rock that forms deep underground from molten magma. Over millions of years, this granite was pushed to the surface by powerful forces within the Earth. Glaciers carved away the surrounding rock, leaving behind the towering cliffs and unique shapes we see today. Even though these landmarks were formed by the same processes, their differences show how nature can create endless variety from the same materials.

Half Dome and El Capitan also play important roles in Yosemite's ecosystem. Their cliffs provide nesting sites for birds like peregrine falcons, which are some of the fastest animals on the planet. These birds dive through the air at incredible speeds, hunting smaller birds and rodents. The cliffs also influence the flow of water in the valley, directing streams and waterfalls that bring life to the plants and animals below.

Yosemite Falls

Yosemite Falls is made up of three sections, each with its own personality. At the very top is the Upper Fall, where the water takes its first big leap, dropping an incredible 1,430 feet. To give you an idea of how high that is, imagine stacking about 10 Statues of Liberty on top of each other—that's how far the water falls. Watching it from below, it looks like the water is flying off the cliff, almost like it's trying to defy gravity.

Below the Upper Fall is the Middle Cascades, a series of smaller, rocky drops where the water churns and crashes its way down. These cascades might not be as tall as the other sections, but they add a wild, unpredictable energy to the waterfall. It's like the water can't decide which way to go and just tumbles wherever the rocks guide it.

Finally, there's the Lower Fall, a shorter but still impressive drop of 320 feet. This is the part of Yosemite Falls that's easiest to reach. A short trail leads you right to its base, where you can feel the mist on your face and hear the roar of the water up close. On a sunny day, the mist can create rainbows, turning the entire scene into something out of a dream.

What makes Yosemite Falls even more fascinating is how it changes with the seasons. In the spring, when snow in the Sierra Nevada mountains begins to melt, the waterfall is at its strongest. Millions of gallons of water pour over the cliffs every minute, creating a thunderous roar that can be heard from miles away. The air around the falls feels cool and damp, and the river below rushes with such force that it carries fallen branches and even small rocks downstream.

By late summer, however, Yosemite Falls often dries up completely. The roaring waterfall becomes a quiet cliff face, and visitors might be surprised to find no water at all. But this seasonal change is part of what makes Yosemite Falls so special—it's a reminder of how connected it is to the rhythms of nature. The snow that melts into water, the rivers that flow through the valley, and even the dry summer heat all play a role in shaping the falls.

For centuries, Yosemite Falls has been more than

just a beautiful sight—it's been a source of inspiration and wonder. The Native American tribes who lived in the valley believed the falls were home to spirits. According to one legend, a tribe of water spirits called the Poloti lived in the pool at the base of the falls. These spirits were said to be powerful and protective, and the falls were considered a sacred place.

When European settlers first arrived in Yosemite in the mid-1800s, they were stunned by the beauty of Yosemite Falls. Artists and photographers quickly made it one of their favorite subjects, capturing its power and majesty in paintings and early photographs. These images helped introduce Yosemite to the rest of the world, convincing people that this was a place worth protecting.

One of the best things about Yosemite Falls is how accessible it is. Whether you're hiking to the top of the Upper Fall, strolling to the base of the Lower Fall, or just admiring it from a distance, there's a way for everyone to experience its beauty. The views change depending on where you stand. From the valley floor, you can see the entire waterfall, its three sections flowing together like a natural staircase. From Glacier Point, you get a bird's-eye view, looking down on the falls as they pour into the valley below.

For those who love a challenge, the hike to the top of Yosemite Falls is an adventure like no other. The trail is steep and strenuous, climbing nearly 3,000 feet in just a few miles. Along the way, hikers pass through shaded forests, rocky switchbacks, and viewpoints that offer stunning glimpses of the valley. Reaching the top is no small feat, but the view is unforgettable. Standing at the edge of the Upper Fall, you can feel the power of the water as it rushes past you and plunges into the void. It's both thrilling and humbling, a reminder of the raw force of nature.

Glacier Point

Perched at over 7,200 feet above sea level, Glacier Point offers one of the most spectacular views in Yosemite National Park. From here, you can see landmarks like Half Dome, Yosemite Falls, and even the distant peaks of the Sierra Nevada mountains. It's the kind of place that makes you pause, not because you're tired, but because you can't help but take it all in.

The journey to Glacier Point is part of the magic. Whether you drive the winding mountain road, hike the challenging Four-Mile Trail, or arrive on snowshoes in the winter, every path leads to something extraordinary. The road curves through pine forests, each turn revealing glimpses of the granite peaks beyond. When you finally arrive, the view bursts into full focus, and it's hard to decide where to look first.

Half Dome dominates the scene, standing proud and unmistakable. From Glacier Point, you see it from a completely different angle than you do in the valley. Its smooth, rounded face looks like the surface of the moon, while its jagged backside tells the story of the glaciers that shaped it. If you're lucky, you might spot tiny dots moving along the summit—hikers who've braved the cables to reach the top. It's incredible to think about the effort it takes to get there, but from Glacier Point, it's all about admiring the view without breaking a sweat.

To the left of Half Dome, you'll see Yosemite Falls cascading down in its three-tiered glory. Even from this height, you can hear its faint roar, like nature's applause echoing through the valley. The falls look almost delicate from here, a contrast to their powerful presence when you're standing at their base. Watching the water tumble down the cliffs from Glacier Point is a reminder of how small we are compared to the forces of nature.

On clear days, you can see much farther than Yosemite Valley. The peaks of the High Sierra rise in the distance, jagged and snow-capped even in summer. These mountains are the source of Yosemite's rivers and waterfalls, the towering guardians of this incredible landscape. Each one has its own story, carved by glaciers, shaped by time, and standing as a testament to the power of the Earth.

Glacier Point isn't just about the view—it's also a place where history comes alive. In the late 1800s, the area became popular with early tourists, drawn by stories of its unmatched beauty. Back then, getting to Glacier Point wasn't as easy as it is today. Visitors would arrive on horseback or in stagecoaches, enduring long and bumpy rides up the mountain. Despite the journey, the reward was worth it. Many of these early visitors described the view in journals and letters, often struggling to find words to capture its grandeur.

One of Glacier Point's most famous attractions was the Firefall, a nightly event that began in the late 1800s. Each evening, hotel staff at the Glacier Point Hotel would push burning embers off the cliff, creating a glowing waterfall of fire that tumbled down into the valley. People gathered in Yosemite Valley to watch, amazed by the fiery spectacle. While the Firefall was undoubtedly impressive, it wasn't exactly good for the environment, and it was eventually discontinued in the 1960s. Today, nature provides its own light shows at Glacier Point, from golden sunsets to star-filled night skies.

Speaking of night skies, Glacier Point is one of the best places in Yosemite for stargazing. With little light pollution and a clear view of the heavens, the stars seem to multiply as the sun sets. On a moonless night, the Milky Way stretches across the sky like a shimmering river of light. If you bring a telescope—or even just a pair of binoculars—you can spot planets, constellations, and maybe even a shooting star or two. It's easy to feel like you're part of the universe when you're standing under a sky that big.

Glacier Point is also a place where science and

nature meet. The panoramic view provides a perfect vantage point to understand how glaciers shaped Yosemite. Thousands of years ago, massive glaciers flowed through the valley, carving out its iconic U-shape and leaving behind the towering cliffs and polished granite we see today. Standing at Glacier Point, it's easy to imagine those ancient rivers of ice, slowly and steadily reshaping the land over millennia.

How these landmarks were formed by nature

Yosemite's breathtaking landmarks didn't just appear out of nowhere—they are the result of millions of years of incredible natural forces shaping and sculpting the land. Standing in Yosemite Valley today, it's hard to imagine the colossal events that created its cliffs, waterfalls, and domes. Yet every granite face, rushing river, and towering peak tells a story of fire, ice, and water.

The story begins deep underground, where molten rock, called magma, once bubbled and churned. Millions of years ago, during the age of dinosaurs, magma pushed its way toward the surface but didn't quite make it. Instead, it cooled and hardened into granite far below the Earth's crust. Over time, the land above eroded, exposing the granite formations we see today, like El Capitan and Half Dome. These landmarks are made of some of the oldest rock in the world, and their journey to the surface was just the beginning of their transformation.

One of the most powerful forces that shaped Yosemite was ice—lots and lots of ice. During the Ice Age, enormous glaciers covered much of the Sierra Nevada mountains. Imagine rivers of ice, thousands of feet thick, slowly moving through the valleys. These glaciers were so heavy and strong that they carved out the U-shaped Yosemite Valley we see today. As the glaciers moved, they carried rocks and debris, grinding away at the granite beneath them like a giant natural bulldozer.

Half Dome, for example, owes its striking shape to glaciers. Scientists believe that the dome was once a full, rounded mountain. But as glaciers scraped along its sides, they carried away chunks of rock, leaving the sheer face we see today. The jagged edge at the top is a reminder of the immense power of ice to shape the landscape.

El Capitan's smooth, vertical walls are another gift from the glaciers. As the ice flowed past, it polished the granite, creating the sleek, almost glassy surface that climbers now challenge themselves to scale. If you stand close to El Capitan and touch its cool granite, you're feeling the result of thousands of years of ice and pressure.

Water also played a huge role in shaping Yosemite's landmarks. Long after the glaciers melted, rivers and waterfalls continued to carve the landscape.

Yosemite Falls, for example, wouldn't exist without the rivers that flow through the valley. Over thousands of years, water has worn away at the granite, creating the plunging drops and cascades we admire today.

Even though water is softer than rock, it's incredibly powerful when it moves. During springtime, when snow from the Sierra Nevada melts, the rivers swell and rush with enormous force. This rushing water carries sediment and debris, slowly wearing down the granite and deepening the valleys. Each drop of water, no matter how small, plays its part in sculpting the land.

Another important force in Yosemite's history is fire. While fire might sound destructive, it's actually a natural and necessary part of the ecosystem. Before people managed the land, wildfires would regularly sweep through Yosemite's forests, clearing out undergrowth and creating space for new plants to grow. Fire also helps giant sequoias, some of Yosemite's most famous trees, by opening their cones and releasing seeds.

These natural fires contributed to the health of the land, shaping the forests that frame landmarks like Glacier Point. The ashes left behind enriched the soil, allowing new plants to thrive. Without fire, the landscape wouldn't look the way it does today.

Another key factor in Yosemite's formation is the unique combination of its climate and geography. The Sierra Nevada mountains act like a giant weather barrier, capturing moisture from the air and creating a mix of rain and snow that feeds Yosemite's rivers and waterfalls. During winter, snow blankets the higher elevations, and as it melts in the spring, it flows into the valley, fueling the waterfalls that make Yosemite famous.

Even earthquakes have left their mark on Yosemite. The Sierra Nevada mountains are still rising, pushed up by tectonic forces deep beneath the Earth. While these movements happen slowly—just a fraction of an inch each year—they occasionally cause earthquakes that can reshape the land in dramatic ways. Rocks tumble from cliffs, trees shift, and the landscape continues to evolve.

All these forces—magma, ice, water, fire, and tectonic movements—worked together to create Yosemite's landmarks. But nature didn't stop there. Even today, the landscape is still changing. Rocks fall from cliffs, rivers carve deeper paths, and plants grow and die, adding to the cycle of life in the park. The Yosemite you see now isn't exactly the same as it was thousands of years ago, and it won't be the same thousands of years from now.

5

ANIMALS OF YOSEMITE

When you step into Yosemite National Park, it's not just the towering cliffs, roaring waterfalls, and ancient trees that greet you. It's the feeling that the land itself is alive, filled with creatures big and small, all living their own stories. Among these are some of the park's most fascinating residents: black bears, deer, and bobcats. These animals don't just make Yosemite their home—they help shape the wild and magical spirit of the park.

Let's start with Yosemite's most famous furry resident, the black bear. Despite their name, not all black bears are black. In fact, in Yosemite, you might spot one that's brown, cinnamon, or even blond. These bears can weigh anywhere from 150 to 500 pounds, though most you'll see in Yosemite are on the smaller side. They're excellent climbers, using their sharp claws to scale trees with ease, and their sense of smell is so strong they can sniff out food from miles away.

Black bears are curious creatures. If you're hiking in the park, you might spot one from a distance, lumbering through a meadow or foraging for berries. They eat a variety of things, from nuts and fruits to insects and plants, and sometimes even small animals. During the fall, they spend most of their time eating to prepare for winter hibernation. Imagine eating nonstop for months just to sleep through the coldest season—that's the bear lifestyle.

But here's the thing about bears in Yosemite: they've learned that where there are people, there's often food. This has led to a few problems. Bears are incredibly smart, and they've figured out how to break into cars, campsites, and even bear-proof containers when they smell something tasty. That's why park rangers work hard to teach visitors how to keep their food safe and why it's so important to follow the rules about storing snacks.

While bears are the superstars of Yosemite's wildlife, the park is also home to another iconic animal: the mule deer. These graceful creatures are easy to spot, especially in the meadows and open spaces. They get their name from their large, mule-like ears, which swivel like satellite dishes to pick up sounds from every direction. Whether they're listening for predators or just the rustle of leaves in the breeze, those ears are always alert.

Mule deer are herbivores, which means they only eat plants. Their diet changes with the seasons—fresh green shoots in the spring, wildflowers in the summer, and acorns in the fall. Watching a group of deer graze in a meadow can feel like stepping into a postcard. They move with such quiet elegance that it's easy to forget they're constantly on guard.

One of the most magical times to see mule deer is early in the morning or just before sunset. That's when they're most active, nibbling on plants or wandering between the trees. If you're lucky, you might even spot a fawn—a baby deer—with its white-spotted coat blending perfectly into the dappled sunlight. The fawns stick close to their mothers, learning how to navigate the wilds of Yosemite.

Then there's the bobcat, one of Yosemite's most elusive residents. Unlike bears and deer, bobcats are solitary and shy, making them much harder to spot. They're about twice the size of a house cat, with tufted ears, short tails, and a coat that's covered in spots and stripes. Their markings help them blend into the rocky terrain and forest undergrowth, making them masters of camouflage.

Bobcats are expert hunters, and their diet includes small animals like rabbits, squirrels, and birds. They're patient predators, stalking their prey with silent steps before pouncing with incredible speed. While you might not see a bobcat during your visit, you can sometimes spot the signs they leave behind, like tracks in the dirt or claw marks on tree trunks.

What's amazing about these three animals—bears, deer, and bobcats—is how they're all connected to Yosemite's ecosystem. The black bears help spread seeds through their droppings, contributing to the growth of plants and trees. The deer's grazing helps shape the meadows, keeping the grasses from growing too tall and allowing wildflowers to thrive. And the bobcats help control the populations of smaller animals, keeping the balance in check.

Birds

High above Yosemite's towering granite walls, the peregrine falcon rules the skies. Known for its incredible speed, this bird is the fastest animal on Earth. During a hunting dive, called a stoop, a peregrine falcon can reach speeds of over 240 miles per hour—faster than most sports cars. Watching one in action is like seeing a living missile streak through the sky.

The peregrine falcon's sharp eyesight helps it spot prey, like pigeons or small birds, from incredible distances. Once it locks on, the falcon folds its wings and dives, hitting its target with such precision that the smaller bird rarely has time to react. It's not just a display of power—it's a testament to nature's engineering. Everything about the peregrine falcon, from its streamlined body to its strong, sharp talons, is built for speed and efficiency.

But peregrine falcons haven't always soared over Yosemite. At one point, they were nearly wiped out due to the widespread use of a pesticide called DDT. The chemical weakened the falcons' eggshells, causing them to break before the chicks could hatch. By the 1970s, peregrine falcons were considered endangered. Thanks to conservation efforts, including banning DDT and protecting nesting sites, these incredible birds have made a remarkable comeback. Today, they're a symbol of resilience, and Yosemite's cliffs provide a perfect home for them to nest and thrive.

While peregrine falcons dominate the high altitudes, another bird is busy making itself known at eye level: the Steller's jay. With its striking blue feathers and black crest, this bird is impossible to miss. Steller's jays are clever and curious, often hanging around campsites and picnic areas looking for crumbs or shiny objects to steal. They're like the park's resident tricksters, entertaining visitors with their bold and mischievous behavior.

What makes Steller's jays so fascinating is their intelligence. These birds are part of the corvid family, which includes crows and ravens—some of the smartest birds in the world. Steller's jays can solve puzzles, remember where they've hidden food, and even mimic the calls of other birds. Sometimes, they'll imitate the cry of a hawk to scare smaller birds away from food. It's like they have their own bag of tricks for survival.

Despite their playful nature, Steller's jays play an important role in Yosemite's ecosystem. They help spread seeds by burying nuts and forgetting about some of them, allowing new plants to grow. They're also skilled foragers, eating everything from insects to berries. Watching a Steller's jay hop around a meadow or perch on a tree branch is a reminder of how vibrant and lively Yosemite can be.

Of course, peregrine falcons and Steller's jays are just two of the many bird species you might encounter in Yosemite. The park is home to over 250 species of birds, each with its own unique role in the ecosystem. Some, like the tiny Anna's hummingbird, zip from flower to flower, helping with pollination. Others, like the majestic great gray owl, hunt quietly at night, their wings adapted for silent flight.

One of the best ways to experience Yosemite's birdlife is to simply look up. Whether you're hiking through a forest, sitting by a stream, or standing in a wide-open meadow, there's always a chance to spot something incredible in the sky or perched in a nearby tree. On a calm morning, you might see a bald eagle soaring over the Merced River, its sharp eyes scanning the water for fish. In the evening, you could hear the haunting call of a common nighthawk as it swoops through the twilight.

Birds are more than just beautiful to look at—they're vital to the balance of Yosemite's ecosystem. They help control insect populations, spread seeds, and provide food for other animals. They're also a sign of the park's health. A thriving bird population means that Yosemite's forests, meadows, and rivers are doing well too.

Tips for safely observing wildlife

One of the first things to remember when observing wildlife in Yosemite is to give animals plenty of space. It's exciting to see a black bear wandering through the forest or a bobcat slinking through the brush, but they're wild animals, not pets. Getting too close can make them feel threatened, and a scared animal might behave unpredictably. A good rule is to keep a distance of at least 100 yards (the length of a football field) from bears and about 25 yards from smaller animals like deer or foxes. If you need binoculars to see them better, that means you're far enough away.

If you're hiking and spot an animal on the trail ahead, stop and take a moment to observe it from a distance. Watch how it moves, what it's doing, and where it's going. If it seems like it's heading your way, step off the trail and let it pass. It's important to remember that this is their home, and you're a guest in their space. Moving quietly and calmly shows respect for the animal and helps you blend into the natural environment.

One of the best ways to see wildlife is to use your ears as much as your eyes. Animals are often easier to hear than to see, especially birds. If you stand still in a forest or meadow, you might notice the distinct tapping of a woodpecker, the call of a Steller's jay, or the gentle rustle of leaves as a squirrel scurries up a tree. By tuning into the sounds around you, you'll often pick up clues about where animals are and what they're doing.

Carrying a small notebook can make wildlife watching even more fun. You can jot down the animals you see, sketch their shapes, or write about their behavior. Did you spot a peregrine falcon diving toward its prey? Or maybe a mule deer fawn hiding in the tall grass? Writing about these moments helps you remember them, and you might even learn to notice patterns, like which animals come out at certain times of day.

It's important to never feed the animals you encounter, no matter how cute they look. In Yosemite, there's a saying: "A fed bear is a dead bear." This means that when bears or other wildlife get used to human food, they lose their natural fear of people. This can lead to dangerous situations for both the animals and visitors. If a bear becomes too comfortable around humans, it might have to be relocated— or worse, put down. Keeping food out of reach and properly stored in bear-proof containers is one of the simplest ways you can help protect Yosemite's wildlife.

The same rule applies to smaller animals like squirrels, birds, and raccoons. While it might seem harmless to toss a scrap of your sandwich to a begging squirrel, it can actually harm them. Human food doesn't provide the nutrition animals need, and feeding them can make them dependent on people rather than foraging on their own. Plus, wild animals can carry diseases, and it's safer for everyone if they stick to their natural diets.

If you're hoping to see specific animals, timing and location are key. Early mornings and evenings are the best times to spot wildlife, as many animals are most active during these cooler parts of the day. Deer often graze in meadows at sunrise, while owls begin their nightly hunts at dusk. Quiet places near water, like rivers and ponds, are excellent spots to watch birds, frogs, and even the occasional beaver.

Dressing appropriately can also make a difference. Wear clothes in natural colors like green, brown, or gray to help you blend into the surroundings. Bright colors or loud patterns might scare animals away. Moving slowly and quietly is equally important. Sudden movements or loud noises can startle wildlife, causing them to run or fly away before you get a chance to watch them.

Carrying a pair of binoculars or a camera with a zoom lens can enhance your wildlife-watching experience. Binoculars allow you to see details like the feathers of a bird or the way a fox's tail twitches, all without getting too close. If you're taking photos, try not to use a flash, as it can frighten animals. Instead, rely on natural light to capture their beauty.

Sometimes, the best way to see wildlife is to find a quiet spot and simply wait. Animals are more likely to come out when the environment feels calm and safe. Sitting by a meadow, leaning against a tree, or perching on a rock by the river can give you a front-row seat to Yosemite's natural theater. You might see a bear cub following its mother, a coyote trotting through the grass, or a family of ducks paddling across the water.

It's also worth learning a bit about animal tracks and signs. If you don't see an animal in person, you might still find evidence of its presence. Tracks in the mud, claw marks on a tree, or even droppings can tell you which animals have passed through an area. These clues add an extra layer of mystery and excitement to your visit, like solving a puzzle written by nature.

Sometimes, wildlife encounters can be unexpected. Maybe a bobcat crosses your path during a hike, or a bear appears near a campsite. In these situations, staying calm is the most important thing. For bears, make yourself look big by raising your arms and speaking in a firm voice to let the bear know you're there. Slowly back away without turning your back, giving the bear plenty of space to leave. Never run—it can trigger a bear's instinct to chase, even if it doesn't see you as a threat.

Fun animal facts

Black Bears: Not Always Black

Let's start with Yosemite's most famous resident: the black bear. You might picture a big black-coated bear stomping through the forest, but did you know black bears in Yosemite aren't always black? They can be cinnamon brown, blond, or even reddish. These color variations help them blend into their surroundings. A blond bear in a meadow is much harder to spot than a dark bear against the green trees.

Black bears are excellent swimmers and climbers, too. They can climb trees faster than most people can run on flat ground! This skill helps them escape predators or reach high places for food. And speaking of food, black bears have an incredible sense of smell. Their noses are so sensitive they can detect scents up to 20 miles away—imagine smelling a pizza in the next town over!

Deer and Their Magic Antlers

Mule deer are easy to spot in Yosemite's meadows, but their antlers are what make them really impressive. Only male deer, called bucks, grow antlers, and they grow them anew every year! During the spring and summer, their antlers are covered in soft skin called velvet, which supplies nutrients to help them grow. By fall, the velvet dries up and falls off, revealing the hard antlers underneath.

What do they use these antlers for? Mostly to show off! Bucks will spar with one another during mating season, locking antlers in a display of strength. But don't worry—they're not trying to hurt each other, just to prove who's the strongest. After mating season, the bucks shed their antlers, and the cycle starts all over again.

Peregrine Falcons: The Sky's Speed Demons

Peregrine falcons hold a world record: they're the fastest animals on Earth. During a hunting dive, they can reach speeds of over 240 miles per hour. To handle these incredible speeds, peregrines have a special bone structure in their nostrils that helps regulate airflow, preventing their lungs from being overwhelmed.

But it's not just their speed that's impressive. Peregrine falcons are also expert hunters. Their sharp eyesight allows them to spot prey from high above, and their powerful talons make them deadly predators. They're like the superheroes of the bird world—fast, strong, and highly skilled.

Steller's Jays: Nature's Tricksters

Steller's jays are the park's noisy pranksters, and they're as clever as they are bold. They can mimic the calls of other birds and even the sound of a hawk to scare away competitors. Imagine being a tiny bird and suddenly hearing what you think is a hawk nearby—it's no wonder they scatter, leaving the jay to swoop in and grab the food.

These birds are also known for their love of shiny objects. They'll sometimes snatch small, glittering items like coins or foil, much to the amusement (or frustration) of campers. But their playful behavior serves a purpose: it helps them find food and outsmart competitors in the wild.

Bobcats: Masters of Stealth

Bobcats might be hard to spot, but their stealthy nature is what makes them such incredible hunters. These medium-sized cats have fur patterned with spots and stripes, which helps them blend into the rocky terrain and forest shadows. They're mostly nocturnal, meaning they're active at night when their prey—like rabbits and squirrels—is also out and about.

When hunting, a bobcat uses its sharp vision and incredible patience. It can stay perfectly still for long periods, waiting for the right moment to pounce. Once it strikes, its strong jaws and sharp teeth make quick work of its prey.

Great Gray Owls: Silent Hunters

If you're lucky, you might spot a great gray owl in Yosemite's quieter areas. These majestic birds are among the largest owls in North America, but what's truly amazing is their silent flight. Their feathers are specially designed to muffle sound, allowing them to sneak up on their prey without being detected.

Great gray owls have excellent hearing, too. They can hear a mouse scurrying under two feet of snow! This makes them some of the most effective hunters in the animal kingdom, even in harsh winter conditions.

Pikas: Tiny Mountain Survivors

High up in the rocky slopes of Yosemite, you might find a tiny, rabbit-like creature called a pika. These small mammals are incredibly cute and incredibly tough. Pikas don't hibernate in the winter, so they spend the warmer months gathering food to store for the colder season. They create little "haystacks" of grass and flowers, which they dry out and stash in hidden spots.

Pikas are also sensitive to heat. If temperatures rise too high, they can overheat. This makes them great indicators of climate change—scientists study pikas to see how rising temperatures affect mountain ecosystems.

6

PLANTS AND HABITATS
MEADOWS: NATURE'S FLOWER GARDENS

Imagine standing in the middle of a meadow on a warm summer day. The grass sways gently in the breeze, and wildflowers create a rainbow of colors stretching as far as you can see. Yosemite's meadows are some of the most beautiful and important habitats in the park. They might look like simple open spaces, but they're actually full of life, providing food and shelter for countless animals and insects.

One of the most striking things about Yosemite's meadows is the wildflowers. In the spring and early summer, flowers like lupines, shooting stars, and Indian paintbrush bloom in bright purples, reds, and yellows. These flowers aren't just pretty—they're also vital for pollinators like bees and butterflies. If you watch closely, you might see a hummingbird darting between blooms or a butterfly landing delicately on a petal.

Meadows are also home to unique grasses and sedges that can survive the soggy conditions of these low-lying areas. During the spring snowmelt, water floods the meadows, turning them into temporary wetlands. This creates the perfect environment for frogs, salamanders, and even dragonflies to thrive. Deer and black bears often visit meadows to graze or search for food, making these open spaces feel like a natural meeting place for Yosemite's wildlife.

Forests: Giants of the Park

As you leave the meadows and step into Yosemite's forests, the air feels cooler, the light dimmer, and the world quieter. Forests are the heart of Yosemite, with trees that stretch so high it feels like they're holding up the sky. The park is home to several types of forests, each with its own character.

The lower elevations are dominated by oak and pine forests. Black oaks, with their spreading branches and acorn-filled canopies, are a favorite of many animals. Bears, squirrels, and even some birds feast on acorns in the fall. The sugar pine, another common tree in Yosemite, is known for having the longest cones of any pine tree—some can be over a foot long!

As you climb higher into the park, the forests change. Here you'll find groves of towering giant sequoias, including the famous Mariposa Grove. These ancient trees can live for thousands of years, and their thick, fire-resistant bark helps them survive the wildfires that occasionally sweep through the forest. Walking among these giants feels almost otherworldly, like you've stepped into a place where time slows down.

Higher still, you'll encounter mixed-conifer forests, with trees like red firs, Jeffrey pines, and incense cedars. These trees are perfectly adapted to the cooler, snowier conditions of Yosemite's mid-elevations. Their needles stay green year-round, allowing them to keep photosynthesizing even during the winter months.

Alpine Ecosystems: Life Above the Treeline

If you keep climbing, eventually you'll leave the forests behind and enter Yosemite's alpine zone. This is a rugged, windswept world where trees can no longer grow, and life has to adapt to extreme conditions. It might seem barren at first, but take a closer look, and you'll discover that even here, plants find a way to thrive.

Tiny alpine plants, like mosses, lichens, and cushion plants, cling to the rocky ground, their roots finding cracks and crevices to hold onto. These plants grow low to the ground to avoid the freezing winds that whip through the high elevations. Their small size also helps them conserve water, which can be hard to find in this dry, rocky terrain.

Wildflowers like alpine gold and sky pilots add bursts of color to the alpine landscape during the short summer growing season. These plants have adapted to bloom quickly, taking advantage of the few warm months before the snow returns. Seeing these hardy flowers in bloom feels like finding a treasure hidden among the rocks.

Alpine meadows, known as tundra, are another feature of Yosemite's high country. These meadows are smaller and more delicate than the ones in the valley, but they're just as full of life. Tiny grasses and sedges provide food for animals like marmots, which spend their summers fattening up before hibernating through the harsh winter.

How It All Fits Together

What makes Yosemite's plant life so special is how everything is connected. Meadows rely on water from snowmelt, forests provide shade and shelter for countless animals, and alpine plants stabilize the rocky soil high above the valley. Each ecosystem depends on the others, creating a delicate balance that has been shaped by thousands of years of natural processes.

Fire plays an important role in maintaining this balance. While wildfires might seem destructive, they're actually a natural part of Yosemite's ecosystems. Fires clear out dead vegetation, make room for new growth, and release nutrients back into the soil. Certain plants, like the giant sequoias, have even evolved to rely on fire for reproduction. The heat from a wildfire opens their cones, allowing seeds to fall to the ground and grow into new trees.

Wildflowers to look for

Lupine: Purple Spires of the Meadow

Lupines are one of Yosemite's most iconic wildflowers, with their tall, purple-blue flower spikes standing out against the green meadows. If you kneel down to take a closer look, you'll notice that each spike is made up of dozens of tiny, pea-like flowers. These blooms are not just pretty—they're also tough. Lupines can grow in a variety of environments, from lush meadows to rocky slopes, thriving in places where other plants might struggle.

One of the coolest things about lupines is their role as "nitrogen fixers." Their roots have special nodules that house bacteria, which take nitrogen from the air and convert it into a form plants can use. This enriches the soil, helping other plants grow. Lupines don't just decorate the landscape—they help create it.

Indian Paintbrush: A Splash of Fiery Red

It's hard to miss the bright red tips of Indian paintbrush flowers dotting Yosemite's meadows. They look like someone dipped a paintbrush in scarlet ink and dabbed it across the landscape. But those fiery red "petals" aren't actually petals at all—they're modified leaves called bracts. The real flowers are much smaller and tucked within the bracts.

Indian paintbrush has a secret: it's a hemiparasite. This means it latches onto the roots of nearby plants to steal nutrients while still making some of its own food through photosynthesis. It's a clever strategy that helps the paintbrush thrive in tough environments, but it also means this flower relies on its neighbors to survive.

Shooting Stars: Little Magicians

Shooting stars look like they belong in a fairy tale. Their delicate pink or purple petals sweep backward, while their centers point downward, almost like they're shooting through the sky. These flowers are often found near streams or in damp meadows, and their unusual shape makes them a favorite of bumblebees.

When a bumblebee lands on a shooting star, it shakes its body, causing the flower to release its pollen. This process, called buzz pollination, is like nature's version of a magic trick, with the bee and the flower working together to ensure the next generation of shooting stars.

Mariposa Lily: Yosemite's Elegant Beauty

The mariposa lily is one of Yosemite's most delicate and elegant flowers. Its name comes from the Spanish word for butterfly, and it's easy to see why. The flower's three petals form a cup, often white or pale pink with intricate patterns of dots or lines inside. These markings guide pollinators, like bees and butterflies, to the nectar hidden at the flower's center.

Mariposa lilies grow in open, sunny areas, and their simple yet striking design makes them a favorite among wildflower enthusiasts. They're also a reminder of Yosemite's history—the flower has been admired for centuries, first by Native Americans and later by settlers exploring the region.

Sky Pilot: A High-Altitude Survivor

If you're hiking in Yosemite's alpine zones, keep an eye out for the sky pilot. This tiny, purple flower grows in rocky, windswept areas above the treeline, where conditions are harsh and plants have to be tough to survive. The name "sky pilot" comes from its habit of growing so high that it seems to touch the sky.

Sky pilots are masters of adaptation. Their small size helps them stay close to the ground, where they're protected from freezing winds. Their thick, waxy leaves conserve water, and their deep roots anchor them firmly in place. Spotting a sky pilot in bloom feels like finding a little piece of hope in the rugged alpine wilderness.

Monkeyflower: A Cheerful Yellow Friend

Monkeyflowers are like nature's little bursts of sunshine. These bright yellow flowers grow along streams and wet meadows, their trumpet-shaped blooms bobbing gently in the breeze. If you look closely, you might notice the faint resemblance to a monkey's face, which is how they got their name.

Monkeyflowers are important for pollinators like bees and butterflies, but they also have a special relationship with the water. They often grow in areas where the soil is saturated, and their presence can indicate the health of a wetland ecosystem. Watching monkeyflowers sway by a stream reminds us of the close connection between plants and their environments.

Yarrow: The Healer

Yarrow is a common wildflower with a long history of being used as a medicinal plant. Its clusters of tiny white flowers look like lace and can often be found growing in meadows and along trails. Native Americans used yarrow to treat cuts and bruises, and it's still considered a healing herb today.

But yarrow's usefulness doesn't stop there. Its strong scent helps repel insects, making it a natural protector for nearby plants. It's also drought-tolerant, thriving in dry conditions where other flowers might wither.

How plants support the park's animals

In Yosemite National Park, plants and animals are like dance partners, each depending on the other to keep the rhythm of the wild alive. Every tree, flower, and blade of grass plays a role in the lives of the creatures that call the park home. Plants don't just provide food —they offer shelter, protection, and even clues about where animals might be found. Let's explore how Yosemite's plants and animals work together to create a thriving ecosystem.

The Oak Trees and Their Acorn Feast

Imagine walking through one of Yosemite's oak

woodlands in the fall. The ground is sprinkled with acorns, each one a tiny treasure chest of nutrients. For many animals in the park, acorns are a vital food source. Black bears love them, spending hours foraging under oak trees to fatten up before their winter hibernation. Deer also munch on acorns, and squirrels gather them to stash away for later, burying them in hidden spots across the forest floor.

But the story doesn't end with animals eating acorns. Some of the acorns the squirrels forget to dig up grow into new oak trees, continuing the cycle. In this way, squirrels help spread oak trees across the landscape, planting the seeds of the next generation.

Wildflowers and Pollinators

Yosemite's wildflowers aren't just pretty to look at —they're lifelines for pollinators like bees, butterflies, and hummingbirds. When a bee lands on a flower, it collects nectar as food and gets covered in pollen. As it buzzes off to the next flower, it spreads that pollen, helping plants reproduce. This process is called pollination, and it's essential for many of the park's plants to grow and thrive.

Some flowers have special relationships with specific pollinators. For example, the delicate shooting star flower relies on bumblebees for pollination. The bee's vibration causes the flower to release its pollen— a natural partnership that keeps both the plant and the bee thriving.

Hummingbirds, with their fast-flapping wings and

long beaks, are another important pollinator in Yosemite. They dart between flowers like Indian paintbrush and monkeyflowers, sipping nectar and spreading pollen along the way. These tiny birds need the energy from nectar to fuel their incredible speed, and the flowers rely on them to help create the next generation of blooms.

Grasses and Grazers

In Yosemite's meadows, grasses play a starring role in feeding the park's herbivores. Deer graze on tender shoots, while rabbits nibble on the edges of grass patches. Even the tiniest insects, like grasshoppers, depend on meadow grasses for food and shelter.

The connection between grasses and animals doesn't stop at grazing. When herbivores like deer and rabbits eat plants, they become food for predators higher up the food chain, like bobcats and coyotes. This creates a web of life, with plants at its foundation, supporting everything from the smallest insect to the top predator.

Forests: Homes and Hiding Places

Forests in Yosemite are more than just collections of trees—they're entire neighborhoods for animals. Squirrels and chipmunks make their homes in the branches of pines and oaks, storing seeds and nuts in tree hollows. Woodpeckers carve out cavities in tree trunks, which later become nesting spots for other birds like owls.

For larger animals, forests provide shelter and

camouflage. Black bears rest in the shade of tall trees, while deer use the underbrush as a place to hide their fawns from predators. Even the fallen logs on the forest floor are important. They create homes for insects, fungi, and small mammals, turning the forest into a layered community of life.

Alpine Plants and High-Altitude Adaptations

High above Yosemite Valley, in the park's alpine zone, plants have adapted to extreme conditions. Tiny flowers like sky pilots and alpine gold grow close to the ground to avoid freezing winds. These plants provide food for marmots, small furry mammals that scurry among the rocks.

During the short alpine summer, marmots feast on plants to build up enough fat to survive their long winter hibernation. Without the hardy alpine plants, marmots wouldn't have the energy they need to make it through the snowy months. In turn, marmots help alpine plants by spreading seeds as they move from one patch of greenery to the next.

Pine Trees and Their Hidden Helpers

Yosemite's pine trees, like the sugar pine and Jeffrey pine, are famous for their massive cones. These cones hold seeds that many animals depend on for food. Clark's nutcrackers, a type of bird, have a special knack for finding and storing pine seeds. They use their sharp beaks to pry seeds from cones and bury them in caches across the forest.

Just like squirrels with acorns, Clark's nutcrackers

sometimes forget where they've buried all their seeds. The forgotten seeds sprout into new pine trees, helping the forest grow. It's a perfect example of how plants and animals work together to shape Yosemite's landscapes.

Plants as Protective Hiding Spots

For some animals, plants are less about food and more about safety. Tall grasses in meadows give fawns a place to hide while their mothers graze nearby. Birds like the California quail use shrubs as cover to avoid predators. Even small mammals like mice and voles use plants as protective tunnels, darting through thick vegetation to stay out of sight.

7

ADVENTURES IN THE PARK

Yosemite National Park is like a giant playground for anyone who loves the outdoors, and hiking is one of the best ways to explore it. Whether you're wandering through meadows, climbing along rivers, or walking beneath towering trees, each trail feels like its own adventure. The best part? There are plenty of hikes in Yosemite that are perfect for families, offering just the right mix of fun, excitement, and nature's wonders.

Lower Yosemite Fall Trail: A Splash of Adventure

Imagine hearing the roar of rushing water as you approach the base of one of the tallest waterfalls in North America. That's exactly what happens on the Lower Yosemite Fall Trail. This short, easy hike is perfect for families, and it's a great introduction to the wonders of the park.

The trail is a one-mile loop, mostly flat and paved, making it accessible for strollers and young kids. As you walk, you'll pass through a forest of oaks and pines, with glimpses of the towering cliffs above. And then you see it—Yosemite Falls. During the spring and early summer, the water crashes down with incredible force, creating a misty spray that cools the air around you. Kids love standing close to feel the mist on their faces—it's like nature's own splash pad.

If you're hiking in the late summer or fall, the waterfall might be just a trickle or even completely dry, but the views of the granite cliffs are still worth the walk. Along the way, look for signs about the history and geology of the falls, or see how many birds and squirrels you can spot in the trees.

Mirror Lake Trail: Reflections and Rock Giants

The Mirror Lake Trail is another family favorite, offering an easy hike with some of the best views in Yosemite. The trail is about two miles round trip if you go to the lake and back, or five miles if you do the full loop around the lake. Either way, it's a gentle path that follows Tenaya Creek, surrounded by trees and granite cliffs.

The highlight of the trail is, of course, Mirror Lake itself. On calm days, the water reflects the towering peaks of Half Dome and Mount Watkins like a perfect mirror. It's a great spot for family photos or a peaceful snack break. In the spring and early summer, the lake is full from snowmelt, but later in the year, it becomes more of a meadow with a trickling creek running through it.

Kids will love looking for frogs, fish, and dragonflies near the water's edge. The trail also has plenty of spots where they can climb on rocks or explore the sandy shoreline. If you're feeling adventurous, try walking barefoot in the creek—it's chilly, but refreshing!

Bridalveil Fall Trail: A Misty Walk to a Magical Waterfall

If your family loves waterfalls, the short hike to Bridalveil Fall is a must. This trail is only half a mile round trip, making it one of the easiest hikes in the park. The path is paved but can be a bit steep in places, so take your time and enjoy the journey.

As you approach the waterfall, you'll hear the sound of water crashing against the rocks long before you see it. When you get close, you'll notice why it's called Bridalveil Fall—the misty spray creates a delicate veil of water that seems to float in the air. On sunny days, you might even see a rainbow in the mist.

Kids can have fun feeling the spray on their faces or looking for tiny rainbows near the rocks. Just be careful—the rocks near the base of the waterfall can be slippery, so it's best to stick to the trail. This hike is especially magical in the spring when the waterfall is at its peak flow.

Cook's Meadow Loop: A Walk Through the Heart of Yosemite Valley

For families who want an easy, flat hike with incredible views, the Cook's Meadow Loop is a perfect choice. This one-mile loop takes you through a picturesque meadow right in the heart of Yosemite Valley. It's an excellent trail for spotting wildlife, from deer grazing in the grass to birds soaring overhead.

The trail also offers amazing views of Yosemite's iconic landmarks, including Half Dome, El Capitan, and Yosemite Falls. You can take your time and enjoy the scenery, stopping to read the interpretive signs along the way that share stories about the meadow's history and ecology.

Kids will love the open space to run around or the chance to look for frogs and insects near the meadow's streams. If you have binoculars, this is a great spot to use them for birdwatching.

Wawona Meadow Loop: Peaceful and Quiet

If your family is looking for a quieter hike away from the crowds, the Wawona Meadow Loop is a hidden gem. This easy 3.5-mile trail circles a lovely meadow near the Wawona area of the park. It's a flat, dirt path that's perfect for walking, jogging, or even horseback riding.

The Wawona Meadow Loop is a great place to see wildflowers in the spring and early summer. Keep an eye out for mule deer grazing in the meadow or hawks soaring overhead. It's also a peaceful spot to listen to the sounds of nature, from the rustling leaves to the chirping birds.

Because this trail is less crowded than others in Yosemite, it's a wonderful place for families who want a more relaxed hiking experience. Bring a picnic and enjoy a quiet meal surrounded by nature.

Tips for Family Hiking Fun

Exploring Yosemite on foot is an adventure, but it's important to be prepared. Make sure everyone in your group wears comfortable shoes and dresses in layers—the weather in Yosemite can change quickly. Don't forget to pack plenty of water, snacks, and sunscreen, especially if you're hiking during the warmer months.

Camping in the wilderness

There's nothing quite like spending a night under the stars in Yosemite National Park. Imagine falling asleep to the sound of a gentle breeze rustling through the trees and waking up to the chirping of birds and the soft light of the rising sun. Camping in Yosemite is more than just a place to sleep—it's an adventure that brings you closer to nature and fills your days with unforgettable experiences.

Picking the Perfect Campsite

Yosemite offers all kinds of camping options, from organized campgrounds with picnic tables and fire pits to backcountry wilderness spots where it's just you and the stars. For families, starting with a designated campground is often the best choice. Places like Upper Pines Campground in Yosemite Valley are great because they have restrooms, water, and easy access to trails.

If your family is ready for a bigger adventure, you can try backcountry camping. This means hiking into the wilderness and setting up camp far away from roads and crowds. You'll need a wilderness permit and a bit of planning, but the reward is a night surrounded by the quiet beauty of nature. Just imagine roasting marshmallows by a campfire, telling stories, and feeling like you're the only people in the world.

Packing for an Adventure

Before you head out, packing the right gear is important. A good tent is a must—it keeps you dry if it rains and provides a cozy place to sleep. You'll also need warm sleeping bags, especially if you're camping in the higher elevations where it can get chilly at night.

Don't forget about food. Camping meals can be simple and fun. Sandwiches, trail mix, and fresh fruit are great for daytime snacks, and cooking over a campfire is always exciting. You can try roasting hot dogs or making campfire pizzas, but the best part is dessert: gooey, chocolatey s'mores.

Make sure you have a flashlight or headlamp for nighttime and a good map of the area. In Yosemite, it's important to store your food properly—use bear-proof containers or food lockers at your campsite to keep animals (especially curious bears) safe and away from your snacks.

Exploring During the Day

One of the best parts of camping in Yosemite is all the exploring you can do during the day. Your campsite is the perfect base for adventures, whether it's hiking to a waterfall, swimming in the Merced River, or climbing on boulders.

If you're staying near Yosemite Valley, there are tons of trails to choose from. You could take a short hike to Lower Yosemite Fall, where you can feel the mist on your face, or walk to Mirror Lake and look for frogs and fish near the water. For a bigger challenge, your family might try hiking part of the Mist Trail, which takes you past roaring waterfalls and up steep granite steps.

In the evening, back at your campsite, you can relax and talk about the day's adventures. Maybe you spotted a deer in the meadow or saw a peregrine falcon diving through the air. Sharing these moments around the campfire makes them even more special.

Stargazing at Night

One of the most magical things about camping in Yosemite is the night sky. Away from city lights, the stars here shine brighter than you've ever seen. On clear nights, you can see the Milky Way stretching across the sky, a band of light made up of billions of stars.

Stargazing is an activity that doesn't need any special equipment, just a comfy spot to lie down. If you bring a pair of binoculars, you can look even closer, spotting craters on the moon or clusters of stars that look like diamonds. Try finding constellations like the Big Dipper or Orion's Belt, or make up your own stories about the patterns you see.

If you're camping during a meteor shower, you might be lucky enough to see shooting stars. All you need to do is sit back, watch, and make a wish.

Staying Safe in the Wilderness

While camping is full of fun and adventure, it's important to stay safe. Always be aware of your surroundings and stick to marked trails when hiking. Yosemite is home to wild animals, and while most of them will avoid people, it's important to give them space if you see one. If you spot a bear or a deer near your campsite, enjoy the sight from a distance—never try to feed or approach them.

Fire safety is also important. Make sure to keep your campfire small and contained in the fire ring provided at your campsite. Always have water nearby to put out the fire when you're done, and never leave it unattended.

Drinking plenty of water is essential, especially during hikes. Yosemite's dry air and sunny weather can make you thirsty faster than you realize. A reusable water bottle is your best friend in the park.

Exploring rivers and waterfalls

The Merced River: A Ribbon of Adventure

The Merced River is the lifeblood of Yosemite, flowing through the heart of the park and bringing everything around it to life. On a warm day, the river becomes a gathering place, with families cooling off in its clear waters or skipping stones along its banks. There's something magical about dipping your toes into the same water that's carved its way through granite cliffs for thousands of years.

For kids, the Merced River offers endless fun. Imagine building a rock dam in a shallow section, creating tiny pools where minnows dart about. Or picture wading into the cool water with your family, feeling the smooth pebbles underfoot. Along the riverbanks, you'll find sandy spots perfect for picnics, where you can eat lunch while watching dragonflies zip through the air.

One of the best spots to experience the Merced River is near Sentinel Beach. Here, the river slows down, creating calm pools that are ideal for wading. Towering cliffs rise on either side, making it feel like you're in the middle of a giant natural amphitheater. If you're lucky, you might spot a heron standing still in the shallows, waiting patiently to catch its next meal.

Vernal and Nevada Falls: Waterfalls Worth the Climb

If you're ready for a bit of adventure, the Mist Trail

is your gateway to two of Yosemite's most breathtaking waterfalls: Vernal Fall and Nevada Fall. These falls are famous for their power and beauty, and the journey to see them up close is just as exciting as the destination.

The trail starts with a steady climb alongside the Merced River, where the sound of rushing water grows louder with every step. As you approach Vernal Fall, you'll notice something amazing: the air around you starts to feel cool and damp, even on a hot day. This is the mist from the waterfall, carried by the wind and turning the trail into a refreshing escape.

Vernal Fall is a powerful curtain of water that drops 317 feet into the river below. Standing at the base of the fall, it's impossible not to feel its energy. The mist creates rainbows in the sunlight, and the roar of the water drowns out everything else. Kids love running their fingers through the spray or seeing how close they can get without getting completely soaked.

For families with older kids who are up for a challenge, the trail continues to Nevada Fall. This waterfall is even taller, dropping 594 feet in a series of cascades that sparkle in the sunlight. The view from the top is unforgettable—you can see the river winding through the valley below and the surrounding granite peaks stretching into the distance. It's a moment that makes all the climbing feel worth it.

Bridalveil Fall: A Gentle Giant

Bridalveil Fall is one of Yosemite's most famous waterfalls, and it's also one of the easiest to explore. A short, paved trail leads to the base of the fall, where you'll feel the mist on your face as the water crashes down from 620 feet above. The trail is perfect for families with young kids, and the sight of the waterfall is enough to leave everyone in awe.

What makes Bridalveil Fall special is the way it seems to float in the air, like a delicate veil of water. On windy days, the water sways back and forth, creating patterns that seem almost alive. It's a place where kids can let their imaginations run wild, imagining stories about water spirits or hidden treasures behind the falls.

Mirror Lake: Reflections of Beauty

Mirror Lake isn't technically a waterfall, but it's connected to Yosemite's waterways and offers a completely different kind of experience. In the spring and early summer, this seasonal lake fills with snowmelt, creating a perfect mirror that reflects the surrounding cliffs and trees. It's a calm, peaceful spot where you can see Yosemite's beauty doubled in the water.

For kids, Mirror Lake is a chance to explore without rushing. The trail to the lake is easy and flat, making it great for little legs. Once you're there, you can skip rocks, look for fish, or just sit quietly and watch the water. The reflections are so clear that it feels like you could step into another world.

Staying Safe and Respecting Nature

Exploring Yosemite's rivers and waterfalls is exciting, but it's important to stay safe and take care of the environment. Water in the park can be cold and fast-moving, especially during the spring snowmelt. Always stick to designated trails and swimming areas, and never try to climb on wet rocks—they can be slippery and dangerous.

It's also important to respect the plants and animals that depend on Yosemite's waterways. Don't disturb frogs, fish, or other creatures you might see, and make sure to pack out all your trash to keep the rivers and waterfalls clean for everyone to enjoy.

Staying safe while adventuring

Exploring Yosemite National Park is full of excitement—towering cliffs, rushing rivers, and endless trails to discover. But the wild beauty that makes Yosemite so special also comes with challenges. Nature is powerful and unpredictable, and staying safe means being prepared, staying aware, and respecting the environment. Let's dive into the simple things you can do to make sure every adventure in Yosemite is as safe as it is unforgettable.

Prepare Like a Pro

Before you even set foot on a trail or dip a toe in the river, being prepared is your first step toward a safe adventure. Start by dressing the part. Yosemite's weather can change quickly, especially in the higher elevations. Mornings might be chilly, afternoons warm, and evenings cool again. Wear layers so you can adjust as the temperature changes, and don't forget a hat and sunscreen to protect yourself from the sun.

Comfortable shoes are a must. Hiking boots or sturdy sneakers with good grip will keep your feet happy and help prevent slips on uneven terrain. If you're planning to explore rivers or streams, bring water shoes to protect your feet from sharp rocks or slippery surfaces.

Packing a backpack is another key to staying safe. Make sure to include plenty of water, especially if you're hiking. Even on cooler days, staying hydrated is important. Bring snacks to keep your energy up—trail mix, granola bars, or fruit are great options. And don't forget a map or guide of the park. Cell phone signals can be spotty in Yosemite, so having a paper map is a smart backup.

It's also a good idea to pack a small first aid kit. A few band-aids, antiseptic wipes, and tweezers can make a big difference if someone gets a scrape or a splinter. If you're venturing further from the main areas of the park, consider bringing a whistle—it's a simple tool that can help you signal for help if needed.

Know Your Limits

Yosemite is big, and its landscapes can be challenging. Whether you're hiking, climbing, or exploring rivers, knowing your limits is one of the best ways to stay safe. Choose activities that match your family's energy and experience level. A short, flat hike might be perfect for younger kids, while older adventurers might enjoy a longer trail or a steeper climb.

If you start to feel tired, it's okay to take a break. Find a shady spot, drink some water, and enjoy the view. Remember, it's not about how fast or far you go—it's about enjoying the journey. And if the weather changes or the trail seems harder than expected, it's always okay to turn back. Yosemite's beauty will still be there for you to explore another day.

Stay on the Trails

Yosemite's trails are carefully designed to keep visitors safe while protecting the park's delicate ecosystems. Staying on the marked paths isn't just a rule—it's an important way to respect nature and avoid danger. Wandering off-trail might lead you to unstable rocks, slippery slopes, or areas with sensitive plants that could be damaged.

If you're hiking with kids, remind them to stay close and keep an eye on the trail markers. Making a game out of spotting trail signs or landmarks can help keep everyone on track. And if you're near cliffs or steep drop-offs, hold hands and walk carefully—it's better to enjoy the view from a safe distance than risk getting too close to the edge.

Be River-Smart

Yosemite's rivers and waterfalls are some of its most beautiful features, but they can also be unpredictable. During spring and early summer, when snowmelt is at its peak, the water is fast, cold, and powerful. Even shallow streams can have strong currents that make wading or swimming dangerous.

If you're exploring near water, stay on dry, stable ground. Rocks near rivers and waterfalls are often wet and slippery, even if they don't look like it. It's easy to lose your footing, so always move slowly and carefully. And while it might be tempting to climb onto a boulder for a closer look, it's safer to admire the water from a distance.

Swimming areas, like those along the Merced River, are great places to enjoy the water safely. Always check for posted signs about water conditions, and make sure an adult is watching if kids are playing in or near the water. If you're not sure whether a spot is safe for swimming, it's better to ask a park ranger or choose a different activity.

Wildlife: Look, Don't Touch

Seeing animals in Yosemite is one of the most exciting parts of any visit, but it's important to remember that they're wild and should be treated with respect. Whether it's a black bear, a mule deer, or a curious squirrel, keep your distance and never try to feed or approach them.

A good rule of thumb is to stay at least 25 yards away from smaller animals and 100 yards away from bears. If you spot an animal on the trail, give it plenty of space and wait for it to move along before continuing. And if you see a bear, stay calm. Talk quietly, wave your arms to make yourself look big, and slowly back away without turning your back on the bear.

Keeping food and trash stored properly is another way to stay safe around wildlife. Bears and other animals have an incredible sense of smell, and leaving food out can attract them to your campsite or picnic area. Use bear-proof lockers or containers for all food, drinks, and trash, and never leave anything scented unattended.

Be Weather-Wise

Yosemite's weather can change quickly, especially in the mountains. A sunny day can turn into a thunderstorm, or temperatures can drop unexpectedly in the evening. Checking the weather forecast before heading out is a simple way to be prepared.

If you're hiking and notice dark clouds or hear thunder, it's a good idea to head back to lower ground. Lightning is more likely to strike in open or high places, so avoid ridges, cliffs, or tall trees. If you get caught in a storm, find a low, sheltered area and wait for it to pass.

On hot days, staying cool and hydrated is just as important. Wear a hat, apply sunscreen, and take breaks in the shade. Drinking water regularly, even if you're not thirsty, will help keep you energized and ready for more adventures.

Have a Safety Plan

Before starting any activity, it's a good idea to let someone know where you're going and when you plan to be back. Whether it's a park ranger, a friend, or a family member, sharing your plans ensures that someone will know where to look if you run into trouble.

If you're exploring with kids, agree on a meeting spot in case anyone gets separated from the group. A large, easy-to-spot landmark like a big tree or a trail sign works well. Remind everyone to stay calm and stay put if they get lost—help is always on the way.

8
PROTECTING YOSEMITE
GUARDIANS OF NATURE

One of the most important jobs of a park ranger is to monitor the park's ecosystems. Yosemite is home to hundreds of plant and animal species, all of which depend on each other to thrive. Rangers keep track of wildlife populations, making sure animals like black bears, peregrine falcons, and mule deer have healthy habitats. They also watch for signs of trouble, such as invasive plant species or changes in water quality, that could harm the delicate balance of the ecosystem.

Sometimes, rangers act as wildlife rescuers. If an animal is injured or in danger, they step in to help. This could mean anything from freeing a bird tangled in fishing line to relocating a bear that's wandered too close to human areas. Rangers know that protecting animals often means protecting their natural behaviors, too. That's why they work hard to teach visitors how to keep wildlife wild—by not feeding animals, storing food properly, and respecting their space.

Teachers of the Wild

Park rangers aren't just protectors—they're also teachers. They love sharing their knowledge of Yosemite's history, geology, and wildlife with visitors. Have you ever listened to a ranger talk about how Half Dome was formed or why sequoias grow so tall? Their passion makes these stories come alive.

Rangers lead guided hikes, nature walks, and campfire programs where kids and adults can learn about the park in fun and interactive ways. They might show you how to identify animal tracks, explain the science behind Yosemite's waterfalls, or tell you about the Native American tribes who first called this land home. Every conversation with a ranger is a chance to discover something new.

If you've ever wondered how Yosemite became a national park, a ranger can tell you that story, too. They'll explain how people like John Muir fought to protect this land from being turned into farms and logging sites, ensuring its natural beauty would remain untouched. Learning about the park's history can make you feel like part of something bigger—a movement to preserve places like Yosemite for everyone to enjoy.

Emergency Responders in the Wild

Rangers are also the park's first responders. If someone gets lost, injured, or caught in a dangerous situation, rangers are the ones who step in to help. They're trained in first aid, search and rescue, and even firefighting, making them ready to handle just about any emergency.

Imagine hiking in a remote area of Yosemite and twisting your ankle. You'd be glad to know a ranger could help you find your way back or even call for medical assistance if needed. Search-and-rescue missions are a big part of a ranger's job, especially in a park as vast and rugged as Yosemite. They use maps, GPS devices, and their deep knowledge of the terrain to locate missing hikers and bring them to safety.

Rangers also work to prevent emergencies before they happen. They put up signs warning visitors about slippery rocks near waterfalls, check trails for hazards, and remind people to carry enough water on hot days. Their goal is to keep everyone safe while exploring the park.

Protectors of the Past

Did you know Yosemite isn't just about nature? It's also full of history, from ancient petroglyphs carved by Native Americans to log cabins built by early settlers. Rangers play a key role in preserving these cultural treasures. They study and protect archaeological sites, making sure artifacts like tools, pottery, and carvings aren't damaged or taken.

In the Mariposa Grove, where the giant sequoias stand, rangers help protect trees that have been alive for thousands of years. They make sure visitors don't walk too close to the roots, which can be easily damaged. By caring for these historical and natural landmarks, rangers ensure that future visitors will be able to experience the same awe and wonder.

Partners in Conservation

Yosemite's rangers don't work alone. They team up with scientists, volunteers, and other organizations to tackle big challenges like climate change, wildfires, and overcrowding. For example, during fire season, rangers collaborate with firefighters to manage controlled burns, which help reduce the risk of larger, more dangerous wildfires.

Rangers also work with schools and community groups to inspire the next generation of park lovers. Programs like the Junior Ranger Program let kids learn about Yosemite through fun activities, earning badges and certificates along the way. These experiences can spark a lifelong love of nature and a desire to protect it.

How Your Can Help

Protecting Yosemite National Park isn't just a job for park rangers—it's something everyone can help with, no matter how old they are. In fact, kids play a huge role in taking care of national parks like Yosemite. Whether it's keeping the trails clean, learning about the park's ecosystems, or inspiring others to care, every little action adds up to make a big difference.

Let's explore all the ways you can help conserve Yosemite and make sure it stays wild and beautiful for years to come.

Leave No Trace: The Golden Rule of Nature

One of the most important ways to help Yosemite is by following the "Leave No Trace" principles. These are simple guidelines that remind us to take care of the environment while we enjoy it. Think of it as being a good guest in nature's home.

For starters, always pack out what you pack in. If you bring snacks or drinks on a hike, make sure all your wrappers, bottles, and leftovers go back into your bag instead of staying behind on the trail. Even small things like orange peels or crumbs can harm animals if they eat them. Plus, seeing trash in a beautiful place like Yosemite is kind of like finding graffiti on a masterpiece—it just doesn't belong.

You can also leave no trace by staying on the marked trails. This might seem small, but it's a big deal. Walking off-trail can trample plants, disturb animal habitats, and even cause erosion. By sticking to the path, you're helping keep Yosemite's landscapes healthy and strong.

Become a Wildlife Ally

Yosemite is home to all kinds of amazing animals, from tiny frogs to mighty bears. But sharing the park with wildlife means knowing how to respect their space. If you see a deer grazing in a meadow or a squirrel scurrying up a tree, enjoy watching them from a distance. Getting too close can scare animals or make them feel threatened, and that's no fun for anyone.

Another way to be a wildlife ally is to resist the temptation to feed animals. It might seem harmless to toss a chip to a begging squirrel, but human food can actually make animals sick. It can also teach them to rely on people for food, which isn't good for their survival. Instead, let animals find their meals the natural way. You can even spread the word to other visitors about why keeping wildlife wild is so important.

Help Keep Yosemite Clean

One of the easiest ways to make a difference is by picking up litter when you see it. Imagine how much cleaner Yosemite could be if every visitor picked up just one piece of trash. The next time you're walking along a trail or enjoying a picnic, keep an eye out for things like candy wrappers, plastic bottles, or forgotten items. Use gloves or a trash bag to collect them, and toss them into the nearest recycling or garbage bin.

If you're feeling extra motivated, you can join a park cleanup event. These are special days when volunteers come together to remove trash from the trails, rivers, and campsites. It's a fun way to meet other people who love Yosemite and to see how much of a difference teamwork can make.

Learn and Share

Helping Yosemite isn't just about what you do in the park—it's also about what you learn and share with others. The more you know about Yosemite's plants, animals, and history, the more you can teach your friends and family why it's important to protect it.

You can start by reading books, watching documentaries, or visiting museums about Yosemite and other national parks. You might discover cool facts, like how black bears help spread seeds through their droppings or how giant sequoias need fire to release their seeds. Sharing these stories with others can inspire them to care about Yosemite too.

If you like to draw or write, try creating your own Yosemite artwork or stories. Maybe you could write a poem about the waterfalls, draw a picture of a peregrine falcon, or make a comic strip about an animal's adventures in the park. Your creations could spark someone else's love for nature.

Join the Junior Ranger Program

The Junior Ranger Program is one of the best ways for kids to get involved in helping Yosemite. It's like a fun, hands-on class where you can learn all about the park while earning a special badge. You'll complete activities like scavenger hunts, nature journaling, or learning about wildlife safety. By the time you finish, you'll know how to be a true steward of the park.

Junior Rangers also take an oath to protect Yosemite and share what they've learned with others.

It's a badge of honor that shows you're part of a team working to keep the park beautiful and healthy.

Protect the Park from Afar

Even if you don't live near Yosemite, there are plenty of ways to help from home. You could start a recycling project at your school, encourage your friends to use reusable water bottles and bags, or plant a tree in your neighborhood. All of these actions help the planet, and that's good for Yosemite too.

You can also support organizations that work to protect national parks. Some groups raise money to help with things like trail maintenance, wildlife research, and fire recovery. Donating a portion of your allowance or holding a fundraiser with your friends are great ways to contribute.

Be a Role Model

Sometimes, the best way to help is by setting an example. When other people see you taking care of Yosemite, they're more likely to do the same. Whether it's picking up litter, staying on the trail, or talking about why feeding animals isn't a good idea, your actions can inspire others to make good choices.

If you're visiting the park with family or friends, remind them of simple ways to help. You could say, "Hey, let's make sure we have a bag for our trash," or "Did you know it's safer for the animals if we don't feed them?" These little reminders can make a big difference.

Stories of successful conservation efforts

Yosemite National Park is a place of towering granite cliffs, ancient trees, and rushing waterfalls—but it's also a place where people have worked together to protect nature. Behind every trail, meadow, and clear-running river are stories of individuals and communities who stood up to make sure Yosemite's beauty would last for generations. Let's dive into some of the most inspiring tales of conservation in the park's history.

Saving the Peregrine Falcon

There was a time when the skies over Yosemite were missing one of their most incredible flyers—the peregrine falcon. These sleek, fast birds, known for their breathtaking dives, were nearly wiped out by the 1970s because of a pesticide called DDT. The chemical caused their eggshells to become so thin that they broke before the chicks could hatch. By the time DDT was banned, only a handful of peregrine falcons remained in the entire United States.

That's when scientists and park rangers stepped in. A team of conservationists began carefully raising peregrine falcon chicks in captivity. Once the young birds were strong enough to survive on their own, they were released into protected areas, including Yosemite. Park rangers watched over the falcons' nests, making sure they were safe from disturbances and predators.

Today, peregrine falcons are thriving in Yosemite once again. You can spot them soaring high above the cliffs of El Capitan or diving at incredible speeds to catch their prey. Their return is a powerful reminder that, with enough care and effort, even species on the brink of extinction can make a comeback.

The Battle for Hetch Hetchy

Imagine a valley as breathtaking as Yosemite Valley, filled with meadows, forests, and a sparkling river. That was Hetch Hetchy before it was flooded to create a reservoir in the early 1900s. The decision to build a dam there sparked one of the first major debates about conservation in the United States.

John Muir, a naturalist and writer who loved Yosemite, fought passionately to save Hetch Hetchy. He believed that wild places should be preserved for their beauty and inspiration, not turned into resources for cities. Although the dam was eventually built, Muir's efforts weren't in vain. His writings and advocacy inspired the creation of the National Park Service, which now protects places like Yosemite from similar threats.

Hetch Hetchy's story didn't end with the dam. Today, conservation groups are working to explore the possibility of restoring the valley. They believe that, with the right tools and technology, Hetch Hetchy could once again become a haven for wildlife and a place for people to explore. While the project is still a dream, it shows how the fight for conservation is never truly over—it's a story that continues to unfold.

Restoring the Mariposa Grove

The Mariposa Grove is home to some of the largest and oldest trees in the world: the giant sequoias. These trees have stood for thousands of years, but by the early 2000s, they were under threat. Trails, parking lots, and roads built too close to the trees were compacting the soil around their roots, making it harder for the sequoias to get the water and nutrients they needed.

In response, Yosemite launched a massive restoration project to protect the grove. Workers removed pavement, relocated parking lots, and restored natural water flow to the area. They also replaced aging boardwalks with ones designed to protect the trees' fragile roots.

When the Mariposa Grove reopened, visitors were greeted by healthier trees and improved trails. The project didn't just save the sequoias—it also created a more peaceful and natural experience for everyone who comes to marvel at these ancient giants.

Bringing Back the Bears

Black bears have always been an important part of Yosemite's ecosystem, but for a while, their relationship with humans was causing problems. Decades ago, visitors often left food out at campsites, and bears quickly learned to raid trash bins and picnic areas. While this might have seemed harmless at first, it put the bears in danger. Bears that became too comfortable around people often had to be relocated—or worse, euthanized.

To fix this, park rangers launched a campaign to educate visitors about bear safety. They installed bear-proof food lockers at campsites and trailheads, making it nearly impossible for bears to get to human food. Rangers also taught visitors how to store their food properly and what to do if they encountered a bear on the trail.

The results have been incredible. Yosemite's bears are now healthier and less likely to wander into dangerous situations. Visitors are more aware of their role in keeping wildlife safe, and the park has become a better place for both humans and animals.

Protecting the Wildflowers

Yosemite's meadows are like nature's gardens, filled with colorful wildflowers that attract bees, butterflies, and hummingbirds. But over the years, some meadows were damaged by visitors walking off-trail or by invasive plants crowding out native species.

To protect these fragile ecosystems, park staff and volunteers worked together to restore the meadows. They removed invasive plants, replanted native species, and built fences to keep visitors on designated trails. The restoration efforts not only brought back the wildflowers but also helped the animals that depend on the meadows for food and shelter.

Today, walking through a meadow in Yosemite

feels like stepping into a painting. The wildflowers are thriving, and the meadows are alive with the hum of bees and the flutter of butterfly wings.

Fire as a Tool for Renewal

Fire might sound like something to fear, but in Yosemite, it's actually a natural part of the ecosystem. Many plants, like the giant sequoias, need fire to grow. Fires clear out dead vegetation, release nutrients into the soil, and help seeds sprout.

For years, people tried to prevent all fires in Yosemite, thinking it would protect the park. But without fire, the forest became overcrowded with plants, making it more vulnerable to large, destructive wildfires. Rangers and scientists realized that fire could be a tool for renewal if used carefully.

Now, Yosemite uses controlled burns to mimic the natural fire cycle. These small, managed fires clear away dry brush and create space for new plants to grow. It's a delicate balance, but it shows how humans can work with nature instead of against it.

YOSEMITE FUN FACTS AND TRIVIA
YOSEMITE FALLS: A TOWERING WONDER

Let's start with one of Yosemite's most famous features: Yosemite Falls. Imagine water tumbling from a height so great that it almost feels like it's falling from the sky. At 2,425 feet tall, Yosemite Falls is the tallest waterfall in North America and one of the tallest in the world. To give you an idea of how tall that is, it's more than twice the height of the Empire State Building!

Yosemite Falls isn't just one waterfall—it's actually three separate sections working together. The Upper Fall starts the journey, plunging a whopping 1,430 feet into the Middle Cascades, which are a series of smaller, rapid drops. Finally, the water reaches the Lower Fall, which adds another 320 feet to the total height. On a clear day, you can see the entire waterfall from Yosemite Valley, and it's a sight you'll never forget.

The best time to see Yosemite Falls is in late spring when the snowmelt fills the rivers and sends water rushing over the cliffs. By late summer, the flow often slows to a trickle, but the sheer height of the cliffs remains awe-inspiring.

El Capitan: The King of Granite

Another record-breaking feature in Yosemite is El Capitan, a giant granite monolith that towers 3,000 feet above the valley floor. That's taller than three Eiffel Towers stacked on top of each other! El Capitan is famous among rock climbers, who travel from all over the world to test their skills on its nearly vertical face.

But you don't have to be a climber to appreciate El Capitan. Just standing at its base and looking up is enough to make you feel tiny. On sunny days, you might spot climbers scaling its face, their colorful gear standing out against the gray rock. And if you visit in the evening, you might catch the golden glow of the setting sun lighting up the granite.

El Capitan also holds a world record in climbing. In 2017, Alex Honnold became the first person to climb El Capitan without ropes or safety gear, a feat known as free soloing. It took him just under four hours to complete the climb, a record-breaking achievement that left people around the world in awe.

Giant Sequoias: Nature's Giants

If you're looking for something just as impressive as Yosemite's cliffs and waterfalls, head to the Mariposa Grove to meet some of the oldest and largest living things on Earth: the giant sequoias. These trees are so big that standing next to one feels like being next to a skyscraper made of wood.

The Grizzly Giant, one of the most famous trees in Yosemite, is estimated to be over 2,000 years old. That means it was already growing when the Roman Empire was at its height! This massive tree stands about 210 feet tall and has branches thicker than most regular trees. It's not just a tree—it's a living piece of history.

Giant sequoias aren't just tall—they're also incredibly resilient. Their thick bark protects them from fire, insects, and disease, and their cones can stay sealed for years, only releasing seeds when exposed to the heat of a fire. This means that fires, which might seem destructive, actually help sequoias reproduce and continue their legacy.

Half Dome: A Granite Icon

Half Dome is another record-breaking feature that's instantly recognizable. This giant granite dome rises nearly 5,000 feet above Yosemite Valley, with one side that looks like it was sliced cleanly in half. It's a favorite spot for hikers and climbers, and reaching the summit is considered one of the ultimate Yosemite adventures.

For those brave enough to attempt it, the hike to the top of Half Dome involves a steep climb and a final section where you use cables to pull yourself up the rock face. It's a challenge, but the views from the top are unforgettable, offering a 360-degree panorama of Yosemite's peaks, valleys, and forests.

Even if you don't climb Half Dome, its distinctive shape is visible from many parts of the park, making it a favorite subject for photographers and artists. It's not just a rock—it's a symbol of Yosemite's rugged beauty.

The Tioga Road: A Drive Through the Sky

Yosemite's Tioga Road is another record-breaker. It's the highest highway pass in California, reaching an elevation of 9,945 feet at Tioga Pass. Driving along this road feels like traveling through a postcard, with views of alpine meadows, sparkling lakes, and snow-capped peaks.

The road is only open during the warmer months, usually from late spring to early fall, when the snow has melted enough to make it passable. Along the way, you'll pass landmarks like Tuolumne Meadows, Tenaya Lake, and the trailhead to Cathedral Lakes. Each stop offers its own breathtaking views and opportunities to explore.

Yosemite's Caves: Hidden Depths

While much of Yosemite's fame comes from its towering heights, the park also has hidden depths. Beneath the surface are a series of caves, including the famous Yosemite Cave. These caves were formed by flowing water carving through the granite over millions of years, creating intricate tunnels and chambers.

Exploring a cave is like stepping into another world, with cool air, dripping water, and fascinating rock formations. Some caves are home to bats, which play an important role in Yosemite's ecosystem by eating insects. Learning about these underground wonders shows that Yosemite's beauty isn't just above ground—it's below it, too.

Strange natural occurrences

Firefall: A Waterfall of Fire

Imagine standing at sunset, looking at El Capitan, when a waterfall suddenly turns into what looks like a river of glowing lava. That's not a trick of your imagination—that's Firefall. Every year, for about two weeks in February, something magical happens at Horsetail Fall. The angle of the setting sun lines up perfectly with the waterfall, lighting it up in brilliant shades of orange and red.

The result looks like fire cascading down the granite cliff, even though it's just water catching the light. The conditions have to be just right: the sky needs to be clear, the waterfall needs to be flowing, and the timing has to be perfect. This rare phenomenon has become so famous that photographers and visitors from all over the world come to Yosemite just to see it.

The Strange Movement of Glacier Point Rockfalls

Yosemite's cliffs are constantly changing, and one of the quirkiest things about the park is the way rocks sometimes fall from Glacier Point. Rockfalls aren't unusual in Yosemite—they're part of what shapes the valley—but the way they happen can be surprising. Imagine hiking through the forest when you suddenly hear a thunderous rumble. That's a rockfall, and it's nature's way of reshaping the cliffs.

What's strange about Glacier Point rockfalls is how unpredictable they are. They can happen at any time, and they often occur without warning. Scientists believe that water seeping into cracks during the day and freezing at night plays a big role. When water freezes, it expands, forcing the rock apart until it eventually breaks loose. These rockfalls remind us that Yosemite's granite walls are alive, constantly shifting and changing over time.

The Mystery of the Moonbows

Most people have seen rainbows, but have you ever heard of a moonbow? Yosemite is one of the few places in the world where you can witness this rare and magical phenomenon. A moonbow is just like a rainbow, but instead of sunlight, it's created by moonlight. When the moon is full and bright, its light reflects off the mist from waterfalls like Yosemite Falls, creating a glowing arc of color in the night sky.

Moonbows are faint and can be hard to see with the naked eye, but they're worth staying up late for. They're best viewed during the spring when the waterfalls are roaring with snowmelt and the moon is at its fullest. If you're lucky enough to spot one, it feels like catching a glimpse of a secret hidden in plain sight.

The Strange "Shaking" Pinecones

In Yosemite's pine forests, there's an odd sound you might hear if you listen carefully—almost like a gentle rattle or shake. This isn't the wind moving the trees; it's squirrels! These clever creatures climb to the tops of pine trees and shake the cones loose to collect seeds. The shaking sound is them working hard to knock the pinecones to the ground.

Once the cones fall, the squirrels scurry down to retrieve them, stash them in hiding places, and snack on the seeds. It's not just a quirky behavior—it's an important part of the forest's ecosystem. Squirrels help spread seeds that grow into new trees, making them nature's tiny gardeners.

Frazil Ice: A River of Slush

Another strange sight in Yosemite happens during the cold months when temperatures drop below freezing. In creeks and rivers, you might notice what looks like a flow of slushy, icy water. This is frazil ice, and it's not something you see every day.

Frazil ice forms when supercooled water droplets freeze in the air and then clump together on the surface of the river. It creates a thick, slushy layer that moves downstream like a slow-motion wave. Frazil ice is most common in places like Yosemite Creek near the base of Yosemite Falls, and it's a mesmerizing example of how water can transform in unexpected ways.

The Wind-Whistling Caves of Tuolumne Meadows

Up in Yosemite's high country, near Tuolumne Meadows, there are caves and cracks in the granite where the wind creates haunting, whistling sounds. As the wind blows through narrow gaps in the rock, it produces tones that range from low hums to high-pitched whistles. It's almost like nature's version of a musical instrument.

These whistling caves have fascinated hikers and climbers for years, and they're a reminder of how even the simplest forces—like wind—can create something extraordinary. If you're exploring the high country, keep your ears open for this eerie and beautiful sound.

The Giant Slabs That Move

Yosemite's granite cliffs are famous for their massive slabs of rock, but did you know some of these slabs can move ever so slightly? These movements are caused by thermal expansion. During the day, the sun heats the rock, causing it to expand. At night, when the temperature drops, the rock contracts. This daily cycle of expansion and contraction can cause the granite to shift ever so slightly over time.

These tiny movements are usually too small for us to feel, but they're part of the natural process that keeps Yosemite's landscape evolving. Scientists study these movements to better understand how the cliffs form and how to keep visitors safe near rockfall-prone areas.

Quiz

Exploring Yosemite through its incredible facts, towering waterfalls, ancient trees, and quirky natural occurrences has been quite the adventure! Let's put that knowledge to the test and have some fun along the way. Get ready to dive into a quiz that will spark your curiosity and maybe even teach you something new. There's no pressure—just see how much you remember and enjoy the journey!

Question 1: What's the name of the tallest waterfall in Yosemite?

A. Vernal Fall

B. Yosemite Falls

C. Bridalveil Fall

D. Nevada Fall

Think back to the roaring sound of water crashing down hundreds of feet and the mist that cools you on a hot day. Which one of these mighty waterfalls takes the title of Yosemite's tallest? If you said **B. Yosemite Falls**, you nailed it! This spectacular cascade is over 2,400 feet tall, making it one of the tallest waterfalls in North America.

Question 2: What special ability helps black bears survive in Yosemite?

A. They can fly short distances.

B. They can swim and climb trees.

C. They can dig tunnels faster than a person can run.

D. They can camouflage perfectly in meadows.

If you imagined a bear scrambling up a tree or paddling across a river, you're on the right track! The answer is **B. They can swim and climb trees.** Black bears are excellent climbers and swimmers, skills that help them find food, escape danger, and thrive in Yosemite's wilderness.

Question 3: Why do giant sequoias need fire to survive?

A. Fire provides light for the trees to grow taller.

B. Fire scares away animals that eat sequoia seeds.

C. Fire opens the cones, releasing the seeds.

D. Fire keeps the air warm enough for growth.

Did you choose **C. Fire opens the cones, releasing the seeds?** That's correct! Sequoias rely on the heat from fires to open their cones and spread their seeds, making fire an important part of their life cycle.

Question 4: What's the fastest animal in Yosemite?

A. Coyote

B. Mountain lion

C. Peregrine falcon

D. Squirrel

If you pictured a peregrine falcon diving through the sky, you're spot on! The answer is **C. Peregrine falcon.** These amazing birds can reach speeds of over

240 miles per hour during a dive, making them the fastest animals in Yosemite—and the world.

Question 5: What strange natural phenomenon happens at Horsetail Fall in February?

A. The waterfall freezes into an ice sculpture.
B. The water glows orange like lava.
C. The waterfall disappears completely.
D. The water flows upward instead of down.

If you've heard about the "firefall," then you know the answer is **B. The water glows orange like lava.** During late February, when the sun sets at just the right angle, the light hits Horsetail Fall and makes it look like it's on fire. It's one of Yosemite's most magical events.

Question 6: What should you do if you see a bear while hiking?

A. Scream and run as fast as you can.
B. Freeze and pretend to be a rock.
C. Make yourself look big and back away slowly.
D. Offer the bear a snack to distract it.

If you chose **C. Make yourself look big and back away slowly**, great job! Staying calm and giving the bear plenty of space is the best way to handle a wildlife encounter. Never run or feed a bear—it's safer for both you and the bear to keep your distance.

Question 7: What makes Mirror Lake special?

A. It's the coldest spot in Yosemite.
B. It reflects the surrounding mountains like a mirror.

C. It's home to glowing algae at night.

D. It changes color depending on the weather.

Did you guess **B. It reflects the surrounding mountains like a mirror**? Perfect! On calm days, Mirror Lake's surface creates stunning reflections of Yosemite's cliffs and trees, making it a favorite spot for photos and picnics.

Question 8: Which tree species in Yosemite can live for thousands of years?

A. Ponderosa pine

B. Douglas fir

C. Giant sequoia

D. Sugar pine

The answer is **C. Giant sequoia**! These massive trees are among the oldest living things on Earth, with some reaching over 3,000 years old. Imagine all the history they've seen!

Question 9: What should you do with your trash when visiting Yosemite?

A. Bury it in the ground to make it disappear.

B. Leave it near a tree for animals to find.

C. Pack it out and throw it away in a trash bin.

D. Toss it into a river to keep it out of sight.

The best answer is **C. Pack it out and throw it away in a trash bin**. Keeping Yosemite clean helps protect wildlife and ensures everyone can enjoy the park's beauty.

Question 10: What is one way kids can help protect Yosemite from home?

A. Donate to conservation groups.
B. Encourage friends to recycle.
C. Learn about Yosemite's ecosystems.
D. All of the above.

If you picked **D. All of the above**, you're absolutely right! Every action, big or small, helps preserve Yosemite for future generations.

Bonus Fun Fact: Why does Yosemite's granite shine?

Yosemite's granite shines because it contains tiny crystals of quartz, feldspar, and mica. These minerals catch the sunlight, making the cliffs sparkle like they're covered in fairy dust. The next time you see El Capitan or Half Dome, look closely—you might spot the glittering surface!

PLANNING YOUR VISIT
SPRING: THE SEASON OF WATERFALLS

As the snow in the mountains begins to melt, Yosemite comes alive with the sound of rushing water. Spring is the time when the park's waterfalls are at their most powerful, roaring down the cliffs and creating misty rainbows in the sunlight. If you've ever dreamed of standing at the base of Yosemite Falls or feeling the cool spray of Bridalveil Fall, spring is your chance.

The meadows in the valley also start to burst with life. Wildflowers bloom in every color imaginable, painting the landscape in bright hues of purple, yellow, and red. Birds return from their winter travels, filling the air with their songs. It's like the park is waking up from a long nap, and everything feels fresh and new.

Spring is a great time for families because the weather is mild—cool enough for hiking without being too hot. Just be prepared for occasional rain showers and muddy trails. If you're exploring with kids, waterproof boots and rain jackets are good to have on hand.

Summer: Adventure Under the Sun

When summer arrives, Yosemite becomes a hub of activity. Long, sunny days mean there's more time to explore, whether you're hiking, biking, or just relaxing by the river. Families flock to popular spots like Yosemite Valley, Glacier Point, and Tuolumne Meadows to take in the iconic views and enjoy outdoor adventures.

The rivers and lakes are perfect for cooling off. Kids can wade in the Merced River or splash around in Tenaya Lake while parents enjoy the stunning scenery. If you're feeling adventurous, you might even try rafting or fishing. Summer is also a great time to camp, with warm nights that are perfect for stargazing.

But summer in Yosemite also means crowds. Popular trails and viewpoints can get busy, especially in the valley. To beat the rush, plan to start your activities early in the morning or later in the afternoon. And don't forget your sunscreen—those sunny days can be intense!

Fall: Colors and Quiet

As the summer crowds fade away, Yosemite transforms into a peaceful retreat. Fall is a time of golden light and crisp air, with the leaves of black oaks and cottonwoods turning shades of yellow and orange. It's a photographer's dream, with fewer people and more chances to capture the beauty of the park.

Hiking in the fall is a real treat. The cooler temperatures make it easier to tackle longer trails, and the changing colors add a touch of magic to every step. Wildlife is also more active, with deer and bears busy preparing for winter. Keep an eye out for squirrels scurrying around, collecting acorns to store for the colder months.

One of the best parts of visiting in the fall is the quieter atmosphere. It feels like you have the park to yourself, with less noise and more time to soak in the beauty around you. If your family loves a slower pace, fall might be the perfect time for your Yosemite adventure.

Winter: A Snowy Wonderland

When winter blankets Yosemite in snow, the park takes on a completely different personality. The valley becomes a scene straight out of a snow globe, with white-capped cliffs, frosty trees, and icicles dangling from rocks. It's a quieter time of year, but that just adds to the charm.

Families visiting in the winter can enjoy activities like snowshoeing, ice skating, and sledding. Badger Pass Ski Area offers skiing and snowboarding, as well as lessons for kids and beginners. Even a simple walk through the valley feels magical, with the snow crunching underfoot and the air crisp and clear.

Winter is also the best time to see Yosemite's

famous "firefall" at Horsetail Fall. In February, the setting sun hits the waterfall at just the right angle, making it glow like molten lava. It's a sight you'll never forget, but it only happens for a short time, so plan carefully if you want to catch it.

Keep in mind that winter weather can be unpredictable, with snowstorms and icy roads. If you're visiting during this season, make sure your car has tire chains and check for road closures before heading out. Warm clothes and plenty of hot chocolate are also must-haves for a winter trip.

What to bring and how to prepare

Dressing for Adventure

The clothes you wear can make or break your day in Yosemite. The park's weather can change quickly, especially in the higher elevations, so dressing in layers is your best bet. Start with a comfortable base layer, like a T-shirt or a moisture-wicking shirt, and add a sweater or fleece for warmth. Bring a waterproof jacket in case of rain or unexpected mist near the waterfalls.

Comfortable shoes are a must! Choose sturdy sneakers or hiking boots with good grip to handle uneven trails. If you're planning to wade in rivers or streams, pack water shoes to protect your feet from sharp rocks or slippery surfaces.

Don't forget accessories. A wide-brimmed hat and

sunglasses will keep the sun off your face, while a cozy beanie and gloves are handy for cooler mornings or evenings. And no matter the season, sunscreen is a must—Yosemite's high elevations mean the sun's rays are stronger than you might expect.

Packing the Essentials

Your backpack will be your best friend in Yosemite, holding all the essentials you'll need for a day of exploring. Start with water—lots of water! Staying hydrated is key, especially if you're hiking or spending time in the sun. Reusable water bottles or hydration packs are great options.

Snacks are next on the list. Choose easy-to-carry, energy-packed foods like trail mix, granola bars, dried fruit, or nuts. These will keep everyone energized and happy during your adventures. If you're planning a longer outing, pack a picnic with sandwiches, fruit, and other favorites.

Other essentials include a first aid kit (for scrapes, blisters, or bug bites), a map of the park (cell service can be spotty), and a flashlight or headlamp for evening activities. A small, lightweight blanket can be useful for picnics or a quick rest in a meadow.

Preparing for Wildlife Encounters

Yosemite is home to an amazing array of animals, from playful squirrels to majestic black bears. While it's exciting to see wildlife, it's important to keep both animals and people safe. One way to do this is by storing all food, trash, and scented items properly. Use bear-proof lockers or containers provided in the park, and never leave food unattended.

If you're hiking, carry a whistle or bear bell to make noise and let animals know you're coming. This reduces the chances of surprising them on the trail. Teach kids to admire animals from a distance—binoculars are a fun way to get a closer look without getting too close.

Planning for Comfort

Spending a day in Yosemite is exhilarating, but it can also be tiring, especially for younger adventurers. Make sure everyone in your family stays comfortable by planning regular breaks. Look for shaded spots to rest, drink water, and enjoy the scenery.

If you're visiting in the summer, consider bringing cooling towels or a small, portable fan to beat the heat. For cooler months, pack hand warmers and extra layers to stay cozy. Lightweight camping chairs or foldable stools can make waiting for sunsets or stargazing much more enjoyable.

Navigating the Park

Before heading out, take some time to review Yosemite's layout and pick a few key spots you'd like to visit. The park is huge, and trying to see everything in one day is impossible. Focus on one area at a time—like Yosemite Valley, Glacier Point, or Mariposa Grove—and plan your activities around that.

Print a map or download one to your phone before arriving. Many areas of the park have limited cell service, so having a backup is always a good idea. If you're driving, make sure to check the road conditions, especially in winter, when snow or ice can affect access to certain areas.

Activities and Extras

Depending on the season, there are plenty of activities to enjoy beyond hiking. In the warmer months, bring swimsuits and towels for a refreshing dip in the Merced River or Tenaya Lake. For winter visits, pack snow gear for sledding, snowshoeing, or skiing at Badger Pass.

If your family loves photography, don't forget a camera or smartphone to capture the park's stunning landscapes. A lightweight tripod can help with family portraits or long-exposure shots of waterfalls. For budding artists, sketchpads and colored pencils are a great way to document the trip creatively.

Eco-Friendly Tips

Part of enjoying Yosemite is helping to protect it. Bring reusable water bottles, utensils, and food containers to reduce waste. Pack out all your trash, and pick up any litter you see along the way. Small actions like these make a big difference in keeping the park clean and beautiful for future visitors.

If you're camping, stick to the "Leave No Trace" principles. Keep your campsite tidy, use designated fire rings, and avoid disturbing plants or wildlife. Sharing these habits with kids helps them learn how to be good stewards of the environment.

Getting Excited Before You Go

The adventure starts before you even arrive in Yosemite! Spend some time learning about the park's history, wildlife, and famous landmarks. Watch videos, read books, or look at maps together as a family. This builds excitement and helps everyone feel more connected to the places you'll visit.

Encourage kids to come up with their own goals for the trip, like spotting a certain animal, finding a cool rock, or learning the name of a wildflower. These little challenges add an extra layer of fun to the experience.

A checklist of must-see places and must-do activities

Must-See Places

   Yosemite Falls

This towering waterfall is one of Yosemite's most famous sights. At 2,425 feet, it's the tallest waterfall in North America! It's made up of three sections: Upper Yosemite Fall, Middle Cascades, and Lower Yosemite Fall. A short, easy trail takes you to the base of Lower Yosemite Fall, where you can feel the mist on your face and hear the roar of the water. In spring, when the snowmelt is at its peak, the waterfall is an unforgettable force of nature.

   El Capitan

Standing in Yosemite Valley and looking up at El

Capitan is like staring at a giant. This massive granite cliff is one of the most famous rock formations in the world, and it's a magnet for rock climbers. Even if you're not climbing, watching climbers through binoculars or spotting tiny dots that are actually people scaling the wall is an activity kids find fascinating.

Half Dome

Half Dome is another iconic granite peak that you can't miss. Its rounded top and sheer cliff make it stand out against the skyline. While hiking to the top is a serious challenge that requires permits and stamina, families can enjoy incredible views of Half Dome from spots like Glacier Point or Sentinel Bridge.

Glacier Point

Speaking of Glacier Point, this viewpoint offers one of the best panoramas in the entire park. From here, you can see Half Dome, Yosemite Valley, and even some waterfalls in the distance. It's a great spot for family photos, and during the summer, rangers often host stargazing programs here.

Mariposa Grove

Imagine walking among trees that have been standing for thousands of years. Mariposa Grove is home to some of Yosemite's giant sequoias, including the famous Grizzly Giant and the California Tunnel Tree. These trees are so massive it's hard to believe they're real until you see them in person.

Tunnel View

As you drive into Yosemite Valley, Tunnel View is

your grand introduction to the park's beauty. From this spot, you'll see El Capitan on the left, Bridalveil Fall on the right, and Half Dome in the distance. It's one of the most photographed views in Yosemite, and it's easy to see why.

Tuolumne Meadows

For a quieter experience away from the crowds, head to Tuolumne Meadows. This high-elevation area is filled with wildflowers, rivers, and wide-open spaces. It's a perfect spot for a picnic, a stroll, or just lying in the grass and watching the clouds.

Mirror Lake

If your family loves reflections, Mirror Lake is a must-see. When the water is still, it creates a perfect mirror image of the surrounding cliffs and trees. It's an easy hike to get here, and kids will enjoy skipping stones or looking for fish in the water.

Must-Do Activities

Go for a Hike

Whether it's a short walk or a longer trail, hiking is the best way to see Yosemite up close. Try the Lower Yosemite Fall Trail for a quick and easy hike, or the Mist Trail if your family is up for a bit more adventure. For breathtaking views, the Sentinel Dome Trail is a great option.

Have a Picnic in a Meadow

Pack a picnic and head to one of Yosemite's meadows for a relaxing lunch surrounded by nature. Cook's Meadow in the valley and Tuolumne Meadows in the high country are both beautiful spots. Spread out a blanket, enjoy your meal, and keep an eye out for deer or birds nearby.

Explore the Rivers

The Merced River is perfect for families who want to splash around or wade in the water. During the summer, you can even rent a raft and float along a calm section of the river. It's a fun way to cool off while taking in the views of the valley.

Watch the Wildlife

Yosemite is full of animals, and spotting them can be an adventure in itself. Look for deer grazing in the meadows, marmots sunbathing on rocks, or peregrine falcons soaring high above. Just remember to watch from a safe distance and never feed the animals.

Become a Junior Ranger

The Junior Ranger Program is a fantastic way for kids to learn about Yosemite while having fun. You'll complete activities, answer questions, and earn a badge to take home as a keepsake. It's a great way to feel connected to the park and its history.

Stargazing

Yosemite's night sky is stunning, especially if you're away from the lights of the valley. Bring a blanket and head to an open area like Glacier Point or Tuolumne Meadows to gaze at the stars. If you're lucky, you might even catch a meteor shower.

Take a Ranger-Led Program

Rangers are experts on Yosemite, and they love

sharing their knowledge with visitors. Join a guided hike, attend a campfire program, or stop by a visitor center for a talk about the park's geology, wildlife, or history. These programs are often interactive and perfect for kids.

Visit a Historic Site

Yosemite is more than just natural beauty—it's also full of history. Check out the Yosemite Museum to learn about the Native American tribes who first lived here or visit the Pioneer Yosemite History Center in Wawona to see old cabins and a covered bridge.

11
YOSEMITE IN YOUR IMAGINATION
PAINTING YOSEMITE: THE CANVAS OF NATURE

Long before cameras could capture Yosemite's stunning views, artists were painting them. One of the most famous painters of Yosemite was Thomas Moran. Moran's incredible paintings of places like Yosemite Valley and the Merced River were so lifelike that people who had never visited the park felt like they had been there. His work even helped convince Congress to protect Yosemite as a national park.

Imagine the patience it must take to paint Yosemite's details—the sunlight glinting off El Capitan, the mist swirling around Bridalveil Fall, or the shadows stretching across a meadow at sunset. These artists didn't just create art; they told a story about Yosemite's magic, freezing moments in time that could be enjoyed forever.

Even today, you can find artists sitting quietly with

their easels and brushes, creating new works of art inspired by the same landscapes that inspired Moran. Watching an artist bring Yosemite to life on a canvas can make you see the park's beauty in a whole new way.

Writing About Yosemite: Words That Spark Wonder

John Muir's name often comes up when talking about Yosemite. He wasn't just an adventurer—he was a writer who had a gift for describing the park in a way that made readers feel like they were standing there with him. Muir called Yosemite "the grandest of all special temples of nature," and his words captured the feeling of being surrounded by its incredible beauty.

Muir's writings weren't just poetic; they were powerful. They inspired people to care about Yosemite and fight to protect it. He used his words to show the world why places like Yosemite mattered, not just for their beauty but for their role in connecting people to nature.

Other writers, like Harriet Monroe and Gary Snyder, have also drawn inspiration from Yosemite. Poetry, essays, and even children's books have been written about the park, each one offering a new perspective on its wonders. Whether it's a poem about the way light dances on Half Dome or a story about a family hiking through the valley, words have a way of bringing Yosemite to life.

Photographing Yosemite: Capturing the Light

Photography has played a huge role in how the world sees Yosemite, and one name stands out above all others: Ansel Adams. Adams was a photographer who fell in love with Yosemite and spent much of his life capturing its beauty through his camera lens. His black-and-white photos of places like Tunnel View, Half Dome, and the Mariposa Grove are some of the most iconic images of the park.

What made Adams' photos so special was his ability to capture light and shadow. He could make a photograph of a cliff feel as grand and awe-inspiring as standing in front of it. Adams didn't just take pictures; he created art that showed the spirit of Yosemite.

Photography in Yosemite isn't just for professionals like Adams. Every visitor with a camera or smartphone can try to capture the park's beauty. Whether it's a close-up of a wildflower, a panorama of the valley, or a snapshot of a squirrel darting through the trees, photos help us remember the magic of Yosemite and share it with others.

Modern Artists Inspired by Yosemite

Today, Yosemite continues to inspire a new generation of creatives. Digital artists use technology to create vibrant illustrations of the park's landscapes. Musicians write songs that capture the feeling of standing beneath a waterfall or hiking through a forest. Even filmmakers have turned to Yosemite for inspiration, using its dramatic scenery as a backdrop for epic stories.

Yosemite's beauty has also sparked creativity in visitors of all ages. Kids sketch pictures of Half Dome, write poems about the rushing rivers, or create sculptures from sticks and stones found along the trails. Every act of creativity, no matter how small, is a way of connecting to Yosemite's spirit.

Why Yosemite Inspires Creativity

What is it about Yosemite that sparks so much imagination? Maybe it's the way the light changes throughout the day, making the same cliff look completely different in the morning than it does at sunset. Maybe it's the sound of the wind whispering through the trees or the roar of a waterfall after a rainstorm. Or maybe it's the sense of awe that comes from standing in a place that feels bigger than yourself.

Yosemite's landscapes are more than just beautiful—they're alive. They tell stories of how the Earth was shaped, how animals and plants survive, and how people have found meaning here for thousands of years. When artists, writers, and photographers create something inspired by Yosemite, they're adding their own stories to this ever-growing tapestry.

CONCLUSION: YOUR YOSEMITE ADVENTURE AWAITS!

Yosemite is a place where every corner holds something amazing. You could spend hours watching the sun play on El Capitan, its light shifting and changing as the day goes on. Each season brings something different to explore: the rushing waterfalls of spring, the warm meadows of summer, the golden leaves of fall, or the snowy stillness of winter.

But Yosemite isn't just about what you see—it's about how it makes you feel. Standing beneath a giant sequoia, you might feel tiny, but also connected to something ancient and powerful. Sitting by the Merced River, watching it flow past smooth stones, you might feel calm, as though the world has slowed down just for a moment. These are the kinds of experiences that stay with you long after you've left the park.

The People Who Shaped Yosemite

Yosemite's beauty has inspired countless people to protect it and share it with the world. John Muir's words helped convince others that Yosemite was a treasure worth saving, while photographers like Ansel Adams showed its wonders through their lenses. Even today, artists, writers, and visitors continue to be moved by this place, adding their own stories to its history.

And it's not just about the people who visit Yosemite—it's also about the people who call it home. The Ahwahneechee, the Miwok, and other Native American tribes lived in harmony with this land for thousands of years, honoring its resources and its spirit. Their connection to Yosemite reminds us to care for the places we love.

The Wild Side of Yosemite

Nature is alive in Yosemite, and it's not hard to spot. From black bears wandering through the forest to tiny tree frogs hiding in the grass, the animals of Yosemite are part of what makes the park so special. Every birdcall, rustling leaf, or ripple in the water is a reminder that this place belongs to more than just humans.

Even the plants have stories to tell. The giant sequoias in Mariposa Grove have stood for thousands of years, watching the seasons change and surviving countless challenges. Meadows bloom with wildflowers in the spring, and high alpine zones show how life can thrive even in harsh conditions.

Your Adventure is Unique

What makes Yosemite truly magical is that every person who visits has their own adventure. Maybe your adventure is climbing to the top of Sentinel Dome and feeling like you're on top of the world. Maybe it's spotting a deer grazing quietly in the early morning light. Or maybe it's simply sitting by a campfire, listening to the crackling wood and sharing stories with your family.

Each trail you hike, each view you take in, and each memory you make becomes part of your Yosemite story. No two adventures are the same, and that's what makes this place so special. Whether you come back again and again or only visit once, Yosemite leaves its mark on your heart.

Protecting the Magic

As much as Yosemite gives to everyone who visits, it also needs our care. Every time someone picks up a piece of litter, stays on the trail, or stores food safely to protect the animals, they're helping to keep the park healthy and beautiful. It's a team effort, and everyone who loves Yosemite can play a part.

By sharing what you've learned, whether through art, stories, or conversations, you're helping others understand why places like Yosemite matter. Every action, big or small, makes a difference. The park you explore today can remain just as wild and wonderful for future adventurers.

The Adventure Never Really Ends

Even after you leave Yosemite, its magic doesn't go away. The memories you've made will stay with you, popping up in your mind whenever you see a photo of a mountain or hear the sound of a rushing stream. The things you've learned about nature, history, and yourself can inspire you to explore other places or even see your own backyard in a new way.

Yosemite has a way of making you feel connected—to the earth, to the people who came before you, and to the people who will come after you. It's a reminder that we're all part of a bigger story, one filled with beauty, adventure, and endless possibilities.

Your Yosemite adventure isn't just a trip—it's a piece of something much greater. And while this chapter may end, the story of Yosemite and your part in it will keep growing, full of new discoveries, dreams, and memories.

Made in the USA
Las Vegas, NV
05 May 2025

ca1ad1fa-2f02-4675-b2f6-72cb0ba70b02R01